(
PER:

26th July '99

Only those who become
aware can bring about
change

Claire C. Murphy SHCJ.

CALLED
TO BE HUMAN

PERSONAL DEVELOPMENT IN CHRIST

CLAIRE C. MURPHY SHCJ

GILL & MACMILLAN

Gill & Macmillan Ltd
Goldenbridge
Dublin 8
with associated companies throughout the world
© Claire C. Murphy SHCJ 1998
0 7171 2678 1

Print origination by
O'K Graphic Design, Dublin

Printed in Malaysia

A catalogue record is available for this book from the British Library.

1 3 5 4 2

CONTENTS

PREFACE   vii

1. THE GLORY OF GOD IS THE PERSON FULLY ALIVE   1
Facing the years ahead   *Elizabeth*

2. WOMAN, YOU ARE FREE OF YOUR INFIRMITIES   9
Facing change   *Luke 13 = 10-17*

3. BE YOURSELF, BUT MAKE THAT SELF
WHAT GOD WANTS IT TO BE   18
On being affirmative   *Many ? Marthy*

4. THE FAITH THAT MAKES ONE WHOLE   30
Health and lifestyle   *Haemorrage*

5. TO WORSHIP IN SPIRIT AND IN TRUTH   42
Examining inherited attitudes   *Samaritans*

6. THE TRUTH WILL MAKE YOU FREE   54
Understanding assertiveness   *Gentile Woman*

7. THE WORD BECAME HUMAN AND LIVED AMONG US   63
The man Jesus   *Jesus the Nazarene*

8. LOVE OTHERS AS YOU LOVE YOURSELF   77
The sin of low self-esteem

9. MODEL WOMEN   85
Facing up to conflict and confrontation

10. PRAYING WITH FEW WORDS   98
Attentive listening

11. RESURRECTION PEOPLE   111
    Our spiritual dimension

12. VARIOUS APPROACHES TO PRAYER   123
    And additional personal development exercises

NOTES   131

PREFACE

This book is the result of the many happy and faith-deepening sessions I spent with adult groups in various parishes in Dublin during the 1980s and 1990s. As we shared past experiences and reflected on the significance of the changes taking place in church and society, we grew in awareness of the need to question our own long-held opinions and attitudes. Many of us grew in self-confidence as we studied the Gospels in the light of the insights gained by the women Scripture scholars, and experienced a new sense of freedom as we entered into 'the mind of Christ'.

Gospel quotations throughout the book are taken from various translations. Jesus spoke Aramaic, the four Evangelists translated his teachings into Greek. Jerome translated from the Greek into Latin. Until the sixteenth century all translations of the Gospels into English were made from the Latin. So when we read the Gospels in English we are two or three translations away from what Jesus said and did. Each translation has its own emphasis depending on the words chosen. To avoid being dependent on any one translation I encourage the use of several and have quoted from the translations best suited to the context in which they are used. The abbreviations are as follows: *The New Testament of our Lord and Saviour Jesus Christ* (Knox), *The Jerusalem Bible* (JB), *The Good News Bible* (GNB), the *New International Version* (NIV), the *New Revised Standard Version* (NRSV).

1

THE GLORY OF GOD IS THE PERSON FULLY ALIVE

FACING THE YEARS AHEAD

INTRODUCTION

The glory of God is the person fully alive. Such was the great insight of Irenaeus, the theologian who died in AD 200. Reflecting on this insight Teresa Okure SHCJ, a present-day Scripture scholar, says:

> . . . if we really want to know what it means to be human, we can discover it in Jesus. 'He became like us in all things, but sin.' In my view, that 'but' is a crucial one. What the statement signifies is, that Jesus is the only person, who in his own right, lived to the full, our common vocation to be human, as God had originally intended it to be. All the arguments among scholars, as to whether Jesus was truly human, since he did not sin, seem to me to miss the essential point. It is we sinners, not Jesus, who are yet to realise our true and full humanity: as it was intended to be, on being created 'in the image and likeness of God'. (Gen. 1:26–27; see also Eph. 4:13)[1]

This is a lifetime calling and needs the support of a group of like-minded friends in order to bring it to pass.

Continuing her reflection, Teresa Okure writes,

> For us Christians, Jesus Christ is the only valid stand-point, from which we can correctly view life, culture, development, and appreciate and accord to all people including women, their rightful place and role in church and society today. It is only through Christ's vision that we can see women, as God

sees them today. Faithfulness to our vocation in Jesus, challenges us to act today, as Jesus would act.[2]

Luke records that as a boy Jesus grew in wisdom and in body. His was an integrated personality, with a spirituality that imbued his personal development so that he perceived life as a whole. For Jesus the worship of God included striving for social justice. As Rosemary Edet HHCJ has pointed out, 'Wherever there was need or prejudice, Jesus broke through categories, rejected taboos . . . and offered freedom of Spirit as a weapon against oppressive rules and limiting roles.'[3] This attitude of Jesus is seen at its most radical in his relationship with women. He was willing to associate freely with women even in public and he set aside Levitical blood laws in order to bring healing to a haemorrhaging woman. He was prepared to bring ritual uncleanness upon himself when he asked to drink from the water pot of a Samaritan woman. Jesus took women seriously, engaging them in theological discussion on a one-to-one basis. Even the woman in the crowd who praised his mother got a direct personal answer – she was not ignored or treated as a passive hanger-on.

THE WOMEN DISCIPLES
All four Evangelists record that women were included among the disciples of Jesus. Luke tells us that some of the women whom Jesus healed became his disciples and constant companions.

> Jesus travelled through towns and villages, preaching the Good News about the Kingdom of God. The twelve disciples went with him, and so did some women who had been healed of evil spirits and diseases: Mary (who was called Magdalene), from whom seven demons had been driven out; Joanna, whose husband Chuza was an officer in Herod's court; and Susanna, and many other women who used their own resources to help Jesus and his disciples. (Lk. 8:1–3 GNB)

These women seem to have formed their own support group as they set out on their journey with Jesus. Given the social background of the time, it would seem safe to presume that they were older women: women with families now reared, some widowed and now enjoying their own private income. Presumably also these women were not taken advantage of, as Luke later recorded that Jesus condemned those teachers of the law 'who take advantage of widows and rob them of their homes' (Lk. 20:47 GNB). Whenever this group of women is mentioned in the Gospels, Mary of Magdala is always named and placed first, just as Peter is when the men are listed. This would suggest that, whatever her mental illness, manic depression or epilepsy, Mary of Magdala, once cured, was able to exercise her innate leadership qualities.

In Jesus these women had found acceptance and became part of his renewal movement, contributing to the common purse, and gaining a new understanding of God as Jesus interpreted the Scriptures for them. From the start they understood service to be at the core of ministry. They were also able to accept that suffering was part of discipleship, and so remained unfazed right up to Golgotha. 'They had followed Jesus while he was in Galilee and had helped him. Many other women who had come to Jerusalem with him were there also' (Mk 15:41 GNB). Reflecting on this passage Dr Mercy Oduyoye writes:

> They witnessed a friend, teacher, son cut off in the prime of life for not conforming to the established order and they must have seen themselves in him, for they too were not as housebound as society would have expected them to be.[4]

The women disciples had known Jesus as a whole person at ease with his emotions. They had presumably been there when some Pharisees warned Jesus not to enter Jerusalem as Herod was on the look-out to have him killed. Jesus told them to 'Go and tell that fox' that he would finish his work and that it was in Jerusalem prophets met their deaths. Then changing from the macho-mode Jesus looked down on Jerusalem with compassion: 'How many times have I wanted to put my arms round all your people, just as a hen gathers her chicks under her wings, but you would not let me!' (Lk. 13:31–35 GNB). These women knew the many facets of Jesus' personality. They had experienced his compassion before, had seen him initiate conflict, challenge his disciples, weep, rejoice, and be equally at ease in the company of rich or poor, men or women, Jew or Gentile.

A NEW SPIRITUALITY

Today women scripture scholars are exploring the Scriptures anew, aware that passages hostile to women come from a patriarchal mentality. This mentality was expressed by men who from their experience of maleness proclaimed as universal their understanding of what it meant to be human, without acknowledging the validity of the female experience. Preaching against pride, lust and aggression does not help most women to become whole. Many women need to be helped to overcome their self-distrust, their passivity and submissiveness, and their devious survival methods of manipulating others.

Many Christians, men and women, find themselves inhibited by their traditional understanding of the church, yet yearn to enter into a committed partnership in the mission of Christ to the world. They believe religious indoctrination has blunted their spiritual potential and are seeking a spirituality that gives meaning, value and direction to their lives. Church leaders became aware of this change of attitude more than thirty years ago, and in a Vatican II document stated,

> As regards religion, there is a completely new atmosphere that conditions its practice. On the one hand people are taking a hard look at all magical world-views and prevailing superstitions and are demanding a more personal and active commitment of faith, so that not a few have achieved a lively sense of the divine.[5]

Writing on Christian spirituality today, Elizabeth Dreyer says that 'Catholics are invited to see themselves and all creation as expressions of God's image and therefore as sacred. This is what is meant by a sacramental view of reality.'[6] And she adds,

> Action for justice, as the fruit of an authentically lived spirituality, takes many forms – from the immediate alleviation of food and housing needs, the care for AIDS patients, to lobbying for just legislation, to paying a just wage, to improving education, and so on.[7]

This brings us back to the first women disciples, for theirs was a spirituality of active caring, an attitude they saw confirmed by Jesus on many occasions and finally when he washed the disciples' feet. For them this act was not a symbolic gesture but part of the Christ ministry, just as later and true to form the Risen Christ would welcome the weary fishermen with a cooked meal by the lake shore. Christian spirituality is centred around eating, drinking, and sharing together in order to meet human needs.

The whole mystery of the Incarnation is missed if we do not

realise fully that we relate to the world and to each other through the body. For women, whose bodies were for so long considered ritually unclean, it is important to rejoice in femaleness and to emphasise the spiritual dimension of menstruation when the monthly shedding of blood reminds women that they are capable of nurturing new life, in the whole process of conception, birthing and nourishing. A genuine spirituality integrates our lives and makes for wholeness.

OLDER WOMEN

It has been suggested already that the women disciples who accompanied Jesus were probably older women. Before joining these women as they accompanied Jesus during his public life, listened to his teachings and witnessed his approach to ministry, there are two other older women worth remembering.

The first is Elizabeth who appears in a scene beloved of many Christian feminists. She is old, married to the priest Zechariah, barren all her life and now past child-bearing age. But God intervened and she became pregnant. Meanwhile her young, probably teenage, relative Mary had conceived the child Jesus. Both pregnancies were mysterious, and Mary, having been told by God's messenger of Elizabeth's condition, hastened south to be with her. 'Filled with the Holy Spirit' Elizabeth welcomed Mary as the 'mother of my Lord'. In the Matthean record it is suggested that some scandal surrounded the conception of Jesus. Did Mary seek understanding and support from the older woman? Whatever the motive for her journey, these two women were the first to share in the mystery of the Incarnation. God had chosen Mary and Elizabeth to be intimate co-workers in this divine activity. It is the only passage in the Gospels in which two women converse alone. Two women affirming and empowering each other, one young and one old, but both through the power of the Spirit pregnant with future prophets and the voice of prophecy.

After the birth of Jesus, in keeping with the law, Mary and Joseph took the child to the Temple to have him consecrated to God. There they met the old man Simeon who, led by the Spirit, recognised the child as the long-awaited Messiah and spoke of his future to Mary and Joseph. Also in the Temple was Anna, widowed after seven years of marriage and now in her eighty-fifth year. She too recognised her saviour, thanked God and spoke of the child to all those who looked to God to set them free. Note that at eighty-four years of age Anna did not confine herself to a private conversation but proclaimed the good news 'to all the people'. Apart from John the Baptist and, of course, Jesus, she is the only person in the Gospels who is referred to as a prophet.

Elizabeth and Anna were two older women who, through the power of the Spirit, affirmed and strengthened the young Mary in the task that lay ahead of her.

OLDER CAN BE BETTER

For most people old age is fifteen years beyond their present age. For fifteen-year-olds you have reached old age when you are thirty. For the seventy-year-olds it starts around eighty-five!

There are two kinds of ageing. The first is biological and comes gradually as the hair turns grey, the eyes grow dimmer and the top register in hearing is lost. It is time for women to rejoice in the freedom of their post-menopausal years, and when told they look ten years younger to ask: 'Where have you been? This is what the fifty- or seventy-year-old woman looks like in the third millennium!'

The second kind, 'social ageing', is imposed abruptly. For many people, the calendar dictates the day of retirement when they become unemployable and sometimes impoverished. Most have accepted these social attitudes before they become redundant and so they obligingly withdraw. If the present becomes unbearable they live in the past or allow illness to take over. The story is told of one old woman who refused to accept this attitude. When asked by her doctor, 'What can you expect from an eighty-year-old knee?', she replied: 'My other knee is eighty and gives no trouble at all.' A throw-away society scraps people, as well as cars and computers.

This negative attitude towards ageing is fairly recent. In the not-too-distant past and among non-industrialised peoples old age was respected. The old were regarded as resource people. In Afaha Oku village in eastern Nigeria the third-year students of Cornelia Connelly College undertook as a project to write up the history and customs of the area. Once a week they went out in twos to visit the older people and wrote down their memories of events and traditional practices. When one old illiterate woman died, the young graduate supervising the project remarked, 'A whole library has been lost.'

In Western cultures there is a tendency to regard youth as something to envy. Yet young people experience great pressures and anxieties, so much so that the suicide rate worldwide is said to be far higher among the young than the old. The fact that the young tend to go around in apparently carefree groups prevents us from recognising the depths of their loneliness. Teenagers often undergo interior turmoil as they come to terms with their sexuality and prepare to become financially self-supporting. Then outside problems arise as they try to secure a career and a steady relationship. Peer pressure with its unwritten expectations can be unrelenting; it is time to buy a car, to work abroad, to have your own home, to marry. Later, as responsibilities accumulate, dissatisfaction with earlier choices can lead to disillusionment. By forty, one can find oneself in a rut and feel a failure.

As the children start leaving home, tensions may multiply. For the mother with no outside interests it may prove a traumatic period, especially if she feels she is no longer needed, no longer has a life-giving function. The father, on the other hand, may be glad of the financial relief and so tension can arise between the couple. To live the older years disillusioned and begrudging would indeed be the ultimate failure and would prevent people from ever achieving their full human potential. Older people become aware of the fact that their time-span is limited and that the years pass more quickly towards the end. This realisation can be a great stimulus to renewed living.

The Christian commitment means undertaking Christ's mission to bring justice to the poor, to give insight to the spiritually blind, to free the oppressed and give hope to all the people (see Lk. 4:16–21). The retired still have the vote and through political lobbying and activity can help achieve better social conditions for young and old in society.

Does such an active Gospel spirituality come as a challenge or as an affirmation for you?

PAUSE FOR REFLECTION
Scripture says the faith that proclaims 'I believe' but has no actions to prove it, is dead (see James 2:14–26).

Relying on the power of the Spirit, what would you be willing to do towards promoting justice and peace among people?

EXERCISE 1

Sit back and take five minutes to think about a person you know of, living or dead, whose life made a difference for her or his contemporaries and the generations that followed. Pause.

Whether Christian, believer or non-believer, how did this person's actions contribute to the promotion of God's reign on earth?

List the God-given talents you have to offer for the good of our Church and society.

GOSPEL REFLECTION

Take Luke's Gospel and, sitting comfortably, read the account of Mary's meeting with Elizabeth (Lk. 1:39–45).

Read it through slowly.

Read it again letting the scene become vivid for you.

Contemplate the scene in silence for about five minutes, allowing your thoughts to rise freely.

Then ask, 'Divine Spirit, what co-operation do you ask of me?'

Remain in silence, listening to any inspirations arising within you.

Now read Mary's Song (Lk. 1:46–56).

Make its sentiments your own.

Rejoice in your knowledge of Jesus your Saviour.

Recall the blessings you have received, and the great things the Spirit has already accomplished in and through you.

From this day on resolve to be remotivated as you consider the tasks remaining to be brought to completion: the powerless to be empowered, the hungry to be fed, children to be liberated (add your own areas of awareness).

Rejoice and be glad as you face the life ahead of you in which old and young, women and men, Christians and other believers work together to hasten the reign of justice and peace on earth.

CLOSING THOUGHT

Follow Mary's example and find a support person. Find two or more if possible and start a group of co-workers. Or alternatively, as there are many committed groups already involved, join the one that suits your talents and so in union with others act as church for the world.

2

WOMAN, YOU ARE FREE OF YOUR INFIRMITIES

FACING CHANGE

A WOMAN BENT DOUBLE WITH INFIRMITY (LK. 13:10–17)
Luke, and Luke only, recorded the encounter between Jesus and a woman who for eighteen years had been unable to stand upright. It took place in a synagogue on the Sabbath. During synagogue services there were several readings and the readers were expected to comment on the teachings in their particular passage.

On this Sabbath Jesus must have been invited to read, for we are told that he was teaching. When he stopped he looked across towards a woman who was disabled and bowed down. He called out to her, 'Woman, you are freed from your infirmity' (Lk. 13:12 RSV). The English translations of the text vary. Some say Jesus called her over to him. It is not clear if Jesus ignored the regulations and called the woman into the men's section. However, we do know that he broke the taboo against touching a woman, for he laid his hands on her. The *Good News Bible* states that 'she straightened herself up', and her immediate response was to praise God.

The response of the synagogue official was anger at Jesus for healing on the Sabbath. Addressing the people, he said there were six days in which to work, and that no one should seek healing on the seventh. To this Jesus responded with, 'You hypocrites!' He then went on to point out that not one of those present would hesitate to untie his ox or his donkey on the Sabbath and see to its needs; therefore was it not right to untie this 'daughter of Abraham' on the Sabbath and so release her from eighteen years of physical bondage? The people rejoiced at his words while his critics were left in confusion.

Notice that in this scene neither the woman nor any other person asked for her to be healed. Her healing was initiated by Jesus who called out to her directly. He did not consult with the male members of her family. It would seem that he already knew her, or at least knew of her, for he was familiar with the fact that she had suffered for eighteen years. Presumably Jesus could have healed her privately after the service or on another day. But no, he deliberately presented his challenge publicly in a place of worship.

The woman had come quietly and painfully to join with others in prayer. Suddenly Jesus, no doubt concerned for her physical condition, focused the attention of the whole community upon her. He called out those marvellous words, 'Woman, you are freed of your infirmity.' She recognised God as the source of healing and so, co-operating with the empowering Spirit, she straightened herself up and praised God.

The official, upset by Jesus, turned his anger elsewhere and rebuked the people. It was his indirect way of getting at Jesus and the woman who stood side by side as together they shared in the official reprimand. There is often the temptation for those in authority to give priority to the maintenance of general regulations over the needs of the individual. The official was aware that a law was broken and good order threatened; Jesus was aware of a woman's bondage and intervened. The message is clear: for Jesus, human compassion takes precedence over religious observance and devotions.

THE HUNGRY DISCIPLES (LK. 6:1–5, MK 2:23–28, MT. 12:1–8)

Luke, Mark and Matthew record the Sabbath incident in which Jesus was walking through a cornfield with his disciples. When the latter gathered some ears of corn, rubbed them in their hands and ate the grain, they were accused of breaking the Sabbath law. Turning towards their accusers Jesus reminded them of what David did when he and his soldiers were hungry and how they went into God's sanctuary where they took and ate the bread that had been consecrated and set aside for the priest.

According to Matthew, Jesus quoted the prophet Hosea saying: 'I want compassion not sacrifice, the knowledge of God not burnt offerings' (see Hos. 6:6). Mark concluded with Jesus proclaiming that the Sabbath was made for the good of the people, not the people for the Sabbath.

THE MAN WITH THE WITHERED HAND (LK. 6:6–11, MK 3:1–6, MT. 12:9–14)

Following the cornfield incident all three Evangelists describe another Sabbath healing. Again Jesus was in a synagogue teaching. Present was a man with a paralysed hand. According to Luke it was his right hand. Also present were some teachers of the law who had followed Jesus to see if he would heal on the Sabbath. He knew their thoughts and asked: 'What does our Law allow us to do on the Sabbath? To help or to harm? To save a man's life or to destroy it?' (Mk 3:4 GNB). Then Mark tells us Jesus looked around at them in anger yet 'he felt sorry for them because they were so stubborn and wrong. He then said to the man: Stretch out your hand' (Mk 3:5 GNB). To stretch out your hand demands trust, a willingness to take a risk. The man stretched out his hand as bidden and life flowed into it. Enraged, the teachers left the synagogue, went to the members of Herod's party and together they planned to kill Jesus.

Notice that once more Jesus initiated the cure and the confrontation. He challenged legalism, that is, obedience to rules rather than justice with compassion. Christian feminists often focus on the Lucan detail that it was the man's right hand. Biologically the left side of the brain controls the right side of the body, so their emphasis is purely symbolic. The left hemisphere of the brain is the source of rationality while the right hemisphere directs creativity. In making the man whole on his right side Jesus freed him to become a more fully creative human being.

THE CHRIST VISION

Jesus was born, lived and died a Jew. He attended synagogue, travelled regularly to Jerusalem to celebrate the religious festivals and to participate in the Temple worship. He carried out his mission within the structures of Judaism. According to the Gospel accounts much of his teaching took place in synagogues. Yet for Jesus, 'No tradition was too sacred to be questioned. No authority was too great to be contradicted. No assumption was too fundamental to be changed.'[1]

First Jesus called for conversion of heart, for a mind that was compassionate and freed from prejudice. He challenged people to undertake greater personal responsibility for their observance of religious rules, regulations and rituals. For Jesus, laws and regulations were not of equal value:

Woe to you, teachers of the law and Pharisees, you hypocrites!
You give a tenth of your spices – mint, dill and cummin. But
you have neglected the more important matters of the law –
justice, mercy and faithfulness. You should have practised the
latter, without neglecting the former. You blind guides! You
strain out a gnat but swallow a camel. (Mt. 23:23–24 NIV)

Jesus tried to wean people away from the kind of legalistic
attitude towards religion which depends on external observance.
Instead he offered inner transformation through the power of the
Spirit; in other words, a personal life-giving spirituality that brought
about wholeness.

John records how later, when Jesus was again among the people,
he asked: 'Why do you want to kill me?' They answered: 'You are
mad.' But Jesus persisted:

One work I did, and you are all surprised by it . . . you
circumcise on the sabbath. Now if a man can be circumcised
on the sabbath so that the Law of Moses is not broken, why
are you angry with me for making a man whole and complete
on a sabbath? Do not keep judging according to appearances;
let your judgement be according to what is right. (7:20–24 JB)

The Kingdom or Reign of God preached by Jesus was not
territorial but personal and universal, inclusive of Jews and
Gentiles. It meant being purified and empowered by the Spirit, so
that through repentance one is freed to accept God's plan for
human kind. Five hundred years later Mohammed would call it
Islam, which means 'surrender to God', and Muslim, that is 'one
who submits to God'. For years we were taught that 'the Kingdom
of God is within you'. More modern translations question the
'within' and use 'among you' or 'in the midst of you', thus stressing
the inclusive community aspect of the divine power at work.
Around Jesus there formed a faith support community which
would continue the Christ vision by crossing cultural barriers and
promoting a more just society in which the divisions between the
races, classes and sexes would be healed. As Paul explained: 'You
were baptised into Christ so there is no longer any division between
Jew and Gentile, slave and free, male and female. You are all one in
union with Christ' (see Gal. 3:27–28).

If we believe that Jesus is divine, then any abstract notion of God
up beyond the clouds must give way to the enfleshed reality of the

Incarnation. Jesus, our model for how a human should think and act, spent the last years of his life on earth publicly challenging the abuse of religious power. He was politically active, but not in the same way as the Zealots who sought independence from Rome. Jesus sought to free people from all forms of oppressive inhibition, both those which came from within the person and those that came from within the local community.

FACING CHANGE

On those Sabbath days the thoughts of many people were challenged, each was called to take personal responsibility for religious action. For the man and woman touched by Jesus life must have changed radically. If in the past they were tempted to use their disabilities as an excuse for passivity or dependency, they could no longer do so. Attitudes of other people towards them would also have changed. After eighteen years the woman who had been bowed down now stood upright and could again see the stars. The man with the withered hand was no longer paralysed on his right side but was made whole, integrated in body and hopefully in mind. Empowered by the Spirit, both were now capable of taking advantage of the new horizons opened up to them.

All change is scary. Yet the Christian task requires that change be faced with courage and that attitudes which alienate or dehumanise people be challenged and overcome. Today we are living in an era that is undergoing change at a rate hitherto unknown to us.

Let us look back over the two thousand years since Jesus walked this planet. The Roman Empire in which he was born and lived had a stable culture that lasted five hundred years. The skills and wisdom passed down through twenty or more generations was of value to each one. In Europe the medieval era brought its own changes with the Crusades and travel to the East. Its discoveries were of benefit to fifteen or so generations that followed. With the Renaissance the rate of change increased. Christopher Columbus reached America, printing was invented and Luther introduced the Reformation; still many generations could rely on their elders to pass on practical knowledge. Meanwhile the average human life-span had reached fifty years. Then came the Industrial Revolution and the centuries of empire-building East and South. With the invention of the power loom and the development of railways, urban populations grew and family structures changed. The extended family continued to be farm-based in the rural areas, while in towns the nuclear family, unsupported and boxed into terraced houses, became the norm. The objective continued to be stability: the permanent job, life-long marriage, residence within the same community. Parents had the same ambitions for their children.

Notice that these changes came about gradually over several generations. Not so in our own twentieth century. The average life-span in Europe increased to seventy, then eighty years. At the start of the twentieth century, the greatest speed at which a person could travel was that of the fastest horse. By mid-century the speed of light had been overtaken as rockets headed out to visit neighbouring planets. Two world wars changed the class system. The Second Vatican Council obliged the Roman Catholic Church to question itself and all its attitudes in the light of the Gospel. Mass communications broke through ghetto mentalities, empires disintegrated, new independent states emerged, the United Nations Organisation was formed, and the microchip altered business methods so that instant transactions could now encircle the globe. The discovery of antibiotics and mind-aiding drugs, new knowledge of sexual biology, transplant and laser surgery, have all improved our mental and physical well-being. Perhaps the greatest change was brought about by the women's movement which looked suspiciously at attitudes presumed to be in keeping with the laws of nature and found them wanting.

Now, as we approach the end of the century, we find that skills acquired in youth are redundant twenty years later – as is evident in the medical, educational and computer professions. This means that a person's security can no longer depend on external stability such as the permanent job, marriage and residence. The traditional academic, religious, artistic and technical education no longer provides sufficient preparation for young women and men entering the twenty-first century. They need a reservoir of inner security based on the development of a personal spirituality, self-esteem and a capacity to be flexible, plus understanding and skill in maintaining relationships.

Cardinal John Henry Newman who died in 1890 may have sensed an acceleration in the rate of change when he made his famous statement: 'To live is to change and to live well is to change often.' This is the attitude to be passed on to the next generation. But one cannot give what one has not got. This is why alarm bells ring in my mind when I attend adult groups and see 'Youth' on the agenda. I have found that discussing the many problems of youth is a great way to avoid having to face up to the need for change in oneself. 'Ah! But, Claire, they are the future.' They are not only the future, they are the present just as we are. If adults can learn to handle the present with confidence, the future will be well served. Therefore, there is an urgent need for adults to get rid of redundant, outmoded attitudes and to embrace our changing times with informed enthusiasm.

Jesus was very specific about the purpose of his mission: 'I came that they may have life, and have it abundantly' (Jn 10:10 RSV). During his public life, Jesus blessed the young but entrusted the Good News to their elders. So, fearlessly, in the power of the Spirit, let us stand upright and stretch out our hands to others in co-partnership, and consider our personal development as part of our call to reach our full human potential. For me, 'Happiness is . . .' meeting with adults who are willing to explore life and faith anew and to share the insights gained over the years. For behind each adult there is usually an extended family. Most young people lose contact with their priests and teachers but remain in touch with their parents, grandparents, aunts and uncles. The greatest gift we can give a young person today is the listening, compassionate friendship of an adult who is open to change and who radiates mental well-being.

PAUSE FOR REFLECTION
Spiritual values are operative in all areas of daily life.

Choose one attitude and one action of Jesus that makes this fact clear.

EXERCISE 1

Think of your life as a river flowing onwards.

Draw the passage of your life through time and space. Use colours if possible.

Begin on the left-hand side of a sheet of paper and draw a line that follows the twists and turns of your life so far.

Indicate the rough and smooth parts of the journey.

Along the banks on either side indicate the dark and sunny periods. Also the people significant to you on your journey.

When you reach the present, let a faint line continue on.

Consider your drawing and notice the many changes you have already gone through in life.

Look at the faint line going on ahead.

Decide on some change you are going to make now in order to enhance the immediate future.

EXERCISE 2

Print in large letters one of the two sentences spoken by Jesus which speaks most to you.

'WOMAN YOU ARE SET FREE' (Lk. 13:12).

'STRETCH OUT YOUR HAND' (Lk. 6:10).

Stick it to your mirror and let it continue to speak to you during the coming week.

GOSPEL REFLECTION

Choose one of the synagogue scenes in which Jesus healed the woman who was bent double (Lk. 13:10–17), or the man with the useless right hand (Mk 3:1–6).

Open the Gospel at your chosen scene.

Sit back comfortably and relax for a moment.

Read the text through slowly.

Read it through a second time, savouring any phrases that speak directly to you.

Either: Reflect mentally on the passage, thinking over the clear message Jesus gave. Examine your own attitudes to discover if you are a law-and-order person or one who tempers justice with compassion.

Or: Use your imagination to enter into the scene. Identify with one of the characters, Jesus himself, the suffering woman or man, the official, a teacher of the law, a relative of the disabled person, a disciple man or woman, a member of the congregation, or just yourself as a modern-day observer.

Become aware of the heat, the sounds, the colours, the presence of the people.

Listen to Jesus preach and watch him act, let your emotions respond according to the character you have chosen.

Stay in the scene for five or ten minutes.

After this mental or imaginative exercise reflect on the experience for a while. Ask yourself: 'Is my attitude towards religion influenced by rules or is it Spirit-inspired? Do I feel burdened, bowed down in any area of my life? Are there areas of my mind that seem paralysed, unable to function? Am I ready to ask to become whole?'

CLOSING PRAYER
Pray to God your Creator, your Redeemer, your Empowerer.

3

BE YOURSELF, BUT MAKE THAT SELF WHAT GOD WANTS IT TO BE[1]

ON BEING AFFIRMATIVE

AT HOME WITH MARTHA AND MARY (LK. 10:38–42)
Luke alone recorded this incident in which Jesus visited two women friends. He was passing through Bethany, a village two miles north of Jerusalem and far from his native Nazareth in Galilee. We are told: 'a woman named Martha welcomed him into her house' (Lk. 10:38 JB). Her sister Mary sat at his feet and listened to what he said. Martha remonstrated with Jesus, asking him to tell her sister to get up and help her. Jesus responded to Martha, by pointing out that she got preoccupied with too many things but that Mary had understood the one thing necessary.

True friends are both affirmative and challenging. In public Jesus constantly challenged the attitudes of his listeners. Here we meet him in a domestic scene, yet find that even here he is equally outspoken. In private situations, such outspokenness is only effective if the person concerned already knows that she or he is valued and respected. Note that Jesus was equally at home with both sisters, though each responded to him differently; while Martha offered Jesus the hospitality of her home and table, Mary offered the hospitality of her heart and mind.

Martha criticised Mary for not giving priority to household activities, just as today some women criticise those other women who pursue public careers. Most women can identify with Martha. They know that domestic work is a basic essential for the betterment of humanity, yet it is constantly devalued by society as it seemed to be by Jesus on this occasion.

In the National Gallery in Dublin there is a painting of this scene. Brueghel painted the landscape and Rubens the figures.

Jesus is seated outside the house with Mary seated at his feet, and Martha is remonstrating with him. If you lift your eyes off the main characters and peer into the dimness of the house you see a man busy at work in Martha's kitchen! It was painted three hundred years ago.

In the Gospel narrative the emphasis is on Mary. She 'sat at his feet'. This is a Jewish term denoting discipleship, a master/student relationship.

> The picture is that of a rabbi instructing his pupil. The extraordinary feature is that the pupil is a woman. Further still, the text seems to presume that the pose Mary has adopted is not just for the one occasion but that the relationship between Jesus as teacher and a woman as student is something for the future. 'Mary has chosen the better part which *will not* be taken away from her' (NRSV). This is unheard of in Rabbinic Judaism.[2]

Is Jesus again questioning cultural norms? He did not tell Mary to return to the kitchen; instead he affirmed her place among the students of theology. There is a message here for us too. If our discipleship is to be truly Christian we need to take time to study the Word as conveyed to us in the Gospels and their commentaries, in our listening to others and in prayerful reflection. In defending Mary, Jesus was stressing the fact that nourishment of mind and spirit is as essential as food and drink to our human fulfilment. Perhaps too, he was emphasising that hospitality includes talking with and listening to another, no doubt a human need that Jesus shared with the rest of humankind.

MARTHA'S PROFESSION OF FAITH (JN 11:1–54)
The Gospel according to John was written some thirty years after that of Luke and about seventy years after the death and resurrection of Jesus. In it we again meet the family in Bethany. Lazarus is dying and his two sisters send a message to Jesus saying, 'Lord, the man you love is ill.' The text continues, 'Jesus loved Martha, her sister and Lazarus' (Jn 11:4–5 JB). From these two sentences we can get some feel for the closeness of the relationship between Jesus and this family. To be with them in their need Jesus risked going south, much to the distress of his Galilean disciples who reminded him that the last time he was in Jerusalem the religious leaders wanted him stoned. However, seeing his

determination Thomas, the twin, said: 'Let us go too, and die with him' (Jn 11:16 JB).

Before Jesus reached the village, Lazarus was already four days in the tomb. Hearing of his approach, Martha went out to meet Jesus and said: 'I know that, even now, whatever you ask of God, he will grant you'(Jn 11:22 JB). Jesus assured her that her brother would rise again and Martha said yes, at the resurrection on the last day. Then Jesus told her that he was the resurrection and the source of everlasting life. Could she believe this? Yes, she replied, 'I believe that you are the Christ' (Jn 11:27 JB). Martha then fetched Mary, who came to Jesus and threw herself at his feet, weeping. Seeing her tears Jesus also wept and those present said, 'See how much he loved him!' (Jn 11:36 JB). Jesus asked to be taken to the tomb. Martha warned that by now the body would stink but Jesus ordered the grave stone removed. Then in a loud voice he called Lazarus to come forth. He came out and Jesus said: 'Unbind him, let him go free' (Jn 11:44 JB).

Notice that both sisters continue to respond in character. Martha hurried out to meet Jesus, Mary remained grieving with her friends, and Jesus in turn responded to each differently. When Mary wept, he wept, communicating from heart to heart. When the practical Martha mentioned the probable state of the body, Jesus responded from head to head and with a practical action, 'Remove the stone.' There was no need for either woman to change, they continued to be themselves, for the love Jesus offered was unconditional.

Whereas Luke focused on Mary, in this incident John gives centre stage to Martha. She is no longer the busy housekeeper but a mature student debating a point of theology with the Master. The scene indicates that she too must have 'sat at the feet' of Jesus. John presented Martha in the role given to Peter by both Mark and Matthew. When travelling in the northern villages of Caesarea Philippi Jesus asked the disciples, 'Who do you say that I am?' Peter replied, 'You are the Christ' (Mt. 16:16 JB). This was the answer given by Martha. Matthew added that in response to Peter's confession of faith Jesus entrusted him with the keys of the kingdom.

A DISCIPLESHIP OF SERVICE (JN 12:1–11)

In the next chapter John recalled a final episode at the house in Bethany. It was six days before the Passover and Jesus and his disciples were invited to dinner; Lazarus was at table while Martha was 'serving'. Presumably only men were dining, as women normally ate apart, except for the paschal meal. Mary entered the room carrying a jar of expensive nard and proceeded to anoint the feet of Jesus, wiping them with her hair. Judas Iscariot complained, saying the ointment could have been sold and the money given to the poor. John commented that Judas said this not because he cared for the poor, but because he had charge of their common fund and helped himself to the money. Jesus rebuked him: 'Leave her alone' (Jn 12:7 JB). He explained that what she had done was in preparation for his burial.

Just as Mary had annoyed Martha, she now annoyed Judas, and in each incident Jesus affirmed her action. These two understood each other, listened to each other. She alone realised 'his hour' was at hand.

> Critics since Theodore of Mopsuestia (who died in AD 428) believe that Mary was the only person in this whole situation who knew what Jesus' 'hour' was all about. Heart spoke to heart and love spoke to love. Jesus himself understood Mary's silent deed and took up her case which was also his case.[3]

In his defence of her, Jesus made it clear to his disciples that Mary had acquired the greater theological understanding of his role.

There is no suggestion in John's account that Mary's action was penitential – rather, according to Jesus it was prophetic. Mary accepted that the mission Jesus had undertaken would lead to his death. Unlike Peter she did not resist this fact nor earn the rebuke, 'Get behind me, Satan!' (Mt. 16:23 RSV). Washing the feet of guests was the work of women and servants. However, Jesus affirmed the symbolic nature of Mary's act when he washed his disciples' feet at the Last Supper, using this act as a model for the exercise of leadership (Jn 13:1–17). Leadership is service. Martha is described as 'serving'.

By the time John's Gospel was written the word *diakonia* ('to serve') had gained an ecclesial meaning suggesting leadership in the Christian community. The two Gospel writers who mentioned the family in Bethany placed a greater emphasis on the discipleship of the two women than they did on that of Lazarus. Martha was like Jesus in her forthrightness. Mary was like him in being a challenging presence following her inner truth rather than social convention. And Jesus loved them both. Yet though so closely involved with Jesus during his last week on earth, and living as they did so close to Jerusalem, there is no mention of them standing by his cross. Perhaps they were in hiding as the chief priests had plans to kill Lazarus as well (see Jn 12:10).

In a fifteenth-century painting by Fra Angelico, Peter, James and John are asleep in Gethsemane as described by Matthew (Mt. 26:40). But the Franciscan friar added two more figures, those of Martha and Mary. Both are wide awake and Martha is supporting Jesus in his agony, such was the esteem in which these two women were held in earlier centuries. Tradition has it that the family from Bethany moved to Marseilles as missionaries of the Gospel. In keeping with this tradition some artists portrayed Martha preaching the Good News in France. Others painted her holding a key.

THE FOUR ACCOUNTS OF THE ANOINTING OF JESUS
(MT. 26:6–13, MK 14:3–9, LK. 7:36–50, JN 12:1–8)
All four Gospels carry a version of the incident in which Jesus while at a meal had either his head or his feet anointed. We have already looked at John's account in which names are given. Mary of Bethany, the sister of Martha and Lazarus, is named as the anointing woman and Judas as the disciple who objected. Scholars agree that the Lucan version with the sinful woman is in a category of its own and took place in a different theological context. Therefore I will deal first with the incidents as described in Matthew and Mark.

They, as well as John, place the anointing within the week of the Passion. Mark, the oldest Gospel, recorded this incident between two stories of betrayal. He started with the chief priest and the elders plotting the death of Jesus two days before the paschal feast. Jesus was again in Bethany, this time in the house of Simon the leper. Presumably, Simon was a man who had been healed by Jesus. Was he the father of Martha and family? We do not know. Martha is always presented as the leading figure in her home, which leads some to believe that Lazarus was a much younger brother or an invalid. While the meal was in progress a woman entered and anointed the head of Jesus with expensive ointment. The disciples murmured, complaining at the waste and saying that this perfumed ointment could have been sold and the money given to the poor. Jesus asked: 'Why are you bothering her?' (Mk 14:6 GNB). He continued, saying that the woman had prepared his body for burial, and that wherever his Good News was preached her deed would be recalled 'in memory of her'. According to Mark it was this attitude of Jesus that finally sent Judas out to betray him, for we are told that Judas immediately went to the chief priest and negotiated the thirty pieces of silver.

Matthew's account is similar to that of Mark. He too starts with the plot to kill Jesus. The house is again that of Simon the leper in Bethany. The woman anoints the head of Jesus. Those present fail to understand the significance of the gesture and instead are angry at the waste. Again Jesus defends the woman and her action, pointing out that it was in preparation for his burial. As Judas goes out to betray Jesus the disciples still fail to accept the imminence of his Passion.

In each case the anointing was a deliberate premeditated act. This woman did not just happen to have an expensive jar of oil with her; no, she knew what she was doing when she entered Simon's house and performed a ritual act that proclaimed how the role of Jesus was about to unfold.

Teresa Okure maintains that the verb *aphiemi* is not adequately translated by the phrase 'Leave her alone.' It carries, she claims, a stronger meaning and she suggests that a better translation would be 'Stop placing obstacles in her way' or 'Stop harassing her.'[4] On each occasion it was the men in the Jesus community who objected to a woman touching his body. Jesus disowned such taboos. Teresa goes on to say that those male disciples in the church today who oppose women's participation in certain ministries should reflect and ask themselves if they are truly guided by a concern for the will of Jesus or have they, like Judas, some ulterior motive?[5]

Speaking on an early morning Irish radio programme, 'Just a Thought', Betty Maher commented,

> Witness the woman who poured the oil on his head: 'Leave her alone' he said to those who objected; 'She has done what it is in her power to do; she has anointed me for my burial.' That was the mind of Christ. Today, what happens? Today, in the church to which I and the majority in this country belong, it is no longer permissible for a woman to anoint a sick person. And I want to ask the questions: Who took this from women? And why? And when? And what I really want to know is: Where is the mind of Christ in the prohibition?[6]

The fate of the anointing woman became the fate of women in the church. Her prophetic authoritative act was regarded as a domestic task. Though the story was told, its significance was ignored. It was not until the thirteenth century that a picture of the woman anointing the head of Jesus was produced. It appeared in a *Book of Hours*.[7] Throughout the centuries, however, many artists painted the sinful woman washing the feet of Jesus.

The episode recorded by Luke occurred in the early days of the public life of Jesus and was not associated with his death. A Pharisee named Simon invited Jesus to a meal in his home – the place is not given. A woman known as a public sinner entered the house and stood behind Jesus, weeping. She washed his feet with her tears, dried them with her hair, kissed them and anointed them with ointment. This description suggests that the dining arrangements were in the Roman style with long couches placed head first around the table. The men reclined on these couches leaning on their elbows, thus their feet were stretched out behind them. In the Judaism of the time there were two categories of public sinners, prostitutes and tax-collectors – the latter because they were in the employ of the Romans and collected taxes from their fellow Jews. The fact that this woman was labelled a 'sinner' indicates that she was a prostitute. Both types of 'sinners' were ostracised by Jewish society.

Simon wondered at Jesus, thinking that if he was truly a prophet he would know what manner of woman touched him. Looking at Simon, Jesus told of a creditor who forgave two debtors, one 500 denarii and the other fifty. Which, he asked, would have loved the creditor most? The one to whom he pardoned most, Simon replied. You are right. I came to your house but you gave me no water for my feet, no kiss of welcome, no oil for anointing, but this woman has many sins forgiven her because she has loved much. Turning to her, Jesus told the woman that her sins were forgiven.

Here we have another incident in which Jesus is happy to receive the ministrations of women. He allowed the prostitute to handle and kiss his feet; the fact that she was a woman, a sinner, proved no obstacle to his accepting her ministry. He remained passive throughout until he sensed the criticism, then he defended both the woman and himself. Simon saw the woman only as a sinner. Jesus took the 'beam' out of Simon's eye by showing him the shortcomings of his own life. There is a danger here of focusing on the woman as a 'public sinner' instead of on Simon and his judgmental attitudes which were not in keeping with the mind of Christ.

These are the four accounts of the anointing of Jesus. Mary of

Bethany and three unknown women are mentioned, one was a sinner. It is important to note that Mary of Magdala was not mentioned in any of the four accounts. Nowhere in the Gospels was Mary Magdalen referred to as a sinner. She was a woman who had been cured of 'seven demons' (Lk. 8:2 RSV). In the Gospels, possession by demons is understood to refer to mental and sometimes physical illness. The Christian tradition has degraded Mary of Magdala. As she was treated so were all women treated in the church. A woman who was a support to Jesus, and to Mary his mother, who was the leader of the women disciples, has for centuries been presented as the model for all repentant sexual sinners, just as women themselves came to be regarded as the source of most sexual sins.

THE ONE WHO ENCOURAGED

In the scenes with Martha and Mary, Jesus not only liberated Lazarus from stagnation in the tomb, but through his affirmation of Mary he liberated the minds of the two women from stagnating within the confines of the socially acceptable. The one was encouraged in initiating change, the other challenged to consider and accept it.

The ministry of affirmation is the work of the Holy Spirit and was so recognised in the early church. We are told that Joseph, a Levite from Cyprus, became known among the first Christians as Barnabas which means 'the one who encourages' (see Acts 4:36). On hearing of the growing faith among the Gentiles in Antioch the church in Jerusalem sent Barnabas to encourage the new believers. He then went to Tarsus in search of Paul and invited him to share in his ministry. They both became teachers in the Antioch community (see Acts 11:25–26). From there they were sent to preach the Good News throughout Asia Minor. John Mark, a young Jew, accompanied them but early on in the journey returned to Antioch. Some years later, when Barnabas and Paul were setting out on a second missionary journey, Barnabas wanted to include John Mark but Paul refused to give him a second chance. The situation became so contentious that the two decided to separate; Paul travelled with Silas, while Barnabas went with Mark – thus affirming him in his missionary work (see Acts 15:37–40).

ON BEING AFFIRMATIVE

In order to practise the ministry of affirmation it is necessary to have faith in the potential of others and to be able to identify their gifts. It is also useful to have a capacity for patience and a mind open to new ideas. Thus equipped, it is possible to enable others to accept their own inner strength and talents by encouraging their initiatives, supporting them in their first attempts, and withdrawing gradually as they gain confidence. It is part of this ministry to acknowledge and praise the other's success without seeking any credit for oneself.

When difficulties arise, consolation brings only a temporary relief. By affirming others we strengthen their faith in themselves so that when the next difficulty arises they are better prepared to deal with it. Affirmation nourishes self-confidence. To belittle or discourage another is to undermine the salvific work of Jesus and therefore to enter into the area of sin. Yet many children, and young people in religious or priestly training, have been belittled and humiliated by parents and teachers 'for the good of their souls'!

Sinners have been described as people who do not love themselves enough. The Gospels tell us that there are two prime commandments: to love God with all our hearts, and to love others as we love ourselves (Mk 12:29–31). Jesus stated clearly that these three areas of loving are of equal importance; that is, the love of God, others and self. Deep down each one knows that she or he is of value, is worthwhile. By nourishing this innate sense of self-worth we are freed to love others with the very love of God. We are freed from jealousy and envy and are able to recognise and appreciate the giftedness of others. The temptation to belittle or put down another does not arise. The child who has been affirmed in this sense of self-worth has the inner security with which to deal with disappointments and challenges and can look forward to a lifetime of enriching relationships.

In his book *Under the Eye of the Clock* the young Christy Nolan describes the day when he first realised that he was different. Christy is spastic and cannot speak, but very early in life he learned to communicate through eye and head movements. In the book, he gave himself the fictitious name of Joseph Meehan. One morning as he heard the village children playing in the school yard he looked down at his uncontrollable body and then gazed at his mother with the tears rolling down his cheeks. This is how he describes his mother's response and the lasting effect it had on him:

Placing him in his chair she then sat down and faced her erstwhile boy, yes, her golden-haired accuser. Meanwhile he cried continuously, conning himself that he had beaten her to silence. Looking through his tears he saw her as she bent low in order to look into his eyes. 'I never prayed for you to be born crippled,' she said. 'I wanted you to be full of life, able to run and jump and talk just like Yvonne. But you are you, you are Joseph not Yvonne. Listen here Joseph, you can see, you can hear, you can think, you can understand everything you hear, you like your food, you like nice clothes, you are loved by me and Dad. We love you just as you are.' Pussing still, snivelling still, he was listening to his mother's voice. She spoke sort of matter-of-factly but he blubbered moaning sounds. His mother said her say and that was that. She got on with her work while he got on with his crying.

The decision arrived at that day was burnt for ever in his mind. He was only three years in age but he was now fanning the only spark he saw, his being alive and more immediate, his being wanted just as he was.

Dread-filled fretting marked Joseph Meehan's scene that day, but that scene and that day looked out though his eyes for the rest of his life. Comfort came in childlike notions, his clumsy body was his, but molested by mother-love he looked lollying looks at his limbs and liked Joseph Meehan.

Because he liked himself his youth sidled along with the minimum of grumbling.[8]

The book goes on to describe his sometimes hilarious schooldays (at the school earlier attended by members of the pop group U2), his school friends, his family life, his way of managing a computer, the publication of his book of poems *Dam-Burst of Dreams* when he was fifteen years of age, his meeting other writers and finally his studies at Trinity College, Dublin.

On several occasions I have read the above passage to adult groups and never once have I met anyone who had had a similar experience of liking herself even as an adult. For those of us who have had our self-love stunted in childhood it is necessary to undertake a ministry of affirmation to the self.

PAUSE FOR REFLECTION
When you are complimented how do you respond?

Do you put yourself down by making little of your appearance, gifts, achievements, etc?

The extent of your resistance to deserved affirmation indicates the measure of your non-acceptance of your own self-worth.

To belittle one's own God-given gifts, to fail to appreciate and use them is to be not only ungrateful for who one is, but is to be insensitive to those who have greater physical, mental or emotional disabilities yet struggle to live life to the full.

To affirm self or others is a Christlike act.

EXERCISE 1

List positive facts about yourself under the following headings:

> health and physical appearance;
>
> mental ability;
>
> spiritual awareness;
>
> your talents;
>
> your capacity to relate to people;
>
> your practice of empowering others.

Decide on an area you will nourish during the next few weeks.

GOSPEL REFLECTION

Sit back quietly and clear your mind of all persistent thoughts. Breathe deeply. Listen to the rhythm of your breathing until you feel comfortably relaxed.

Now recall the scene in which Jesus is sharing a quiet time with the two sisters. Stay in the scene until you get some sense of the ease with which he related to them.

Move into the scene of bereavement. Observe Jesus as he shares in the sorrow of his friends. Watch Martha as she stands face to face with Jesus discussing the mystery of death and everlasting life.

Finally enter into the last scene of celebration. Martha is 'serving', probably the hostess. Mary enters and carries out her prophetic ritual. Hear the displeasure of those present. Listen to Jesus again affirming her.

Now ask yourself:

Whose 'feet' do I 'wash'?

How do I 'serve'?

When did I last affirm another?

Pray to the all-enlightening Spirit.

CLOSING PRAYER

'It was you who created my inmost self,
and put me together in my mother's womb;
for all these mysteries I thank you;
for the wonder of myself, for the wonder of your works.'
(Ps. 139:13–14 JB)

Continue praying to the all-empowering Spirit.

4

THE FAITH THAT MAKES ONE WHOLE

HEALTH AND LIFESTYLE

THE HAEMORRHAGING WOMAN
(MK 5:25–34, MT. 9:20–22, LK. 8:42–48)
One day while Jesus was teaching near the Sea of Galilee an official of the local synagogue, named Jairus, begged Jesus to come and heal his daughter who was dying. Jesus went with him immediately.

Among the people listening to Jesus was a woman who for twelve years had suffered a slow but constant haemorrhage. She had spent all she had on doctors and now had nothing left. As Jesus passed she stretched out her hand and touched the edge of his garment. On doing so 'she had the feeling inside herself that she was healed of her trouble' (Mk 5:29 GNB). Jesus, knowing that power had gone out from him, turned and asked who had touched him. The disciples pointed out that many people were crowding them but the woman, knowing what Jesus meant, came and fell at his feet. Looking at her Jesus said, 'Courage, my daughter! Your faith has made you well' (Mt. 9:22 GNB). Then he continued on his way.

RELIGIOUS PURITY
According to Levitical law a woman was unclean during her monthly periods. Throughout her period, a person who touched her, a bed she lay on or a chair she sat on, was unclean until evening. If a woman had a flow of blood outside her period the same taboos applied for as long as the flow lasted. If cured she was considered clean after seven days and had to bring two turtle doves and two pigeons to the priest, who would 'offer one for a sin offering and the other for a burnt offering; and the priest shall make atonement on her behalf before the Lord for her unclean discharge' (see Lev. 15). On giving birth to a boy she was unclean

for seven days followed by thirty-three days of 'blood purification'. After the birth of a girl the uncleanness lasted fourteen days and required sixty-six days of 'blood purification'. This meant that daughters started life as a great inconvenience to their mothers. Also during this time the woman was forbidden to touch any holy thing or come into the sanctuary (see Lev. 12:1–12).

These religious regulations caused most women to be considered unclean for the greater part of their lives. 'Since women were menstruants by nature, they could not be relied upon at all times to be ritually clean. For this reason they were barred as a sex for life from sacred places and ministries in Judaism.'[1] Think what being regarded as ritually impure does to a woman's self-esteem.

We know what Jesus thought of ritual purity. He described as hypocrites the religious teachers who insisted on purified cups while within they were full of dishonesty and greed. Earlier he had made it clear to the disciples that it was not the food that was swallowed that made a person unclean but the thoughts and attitudes of mind that led to murder, adultery, theft and slander (Mt. 15:10–20). In his dealings with women Jesus stood firmly opposed to taboos. Did he, when praying Psalm 139, wonder why women's bodies were considered unclean?

> It was you who created my inmost self,
> and put me together in my mother's womb;
> for all these mysteries I thank you;
> for the wonder of myself, for the wonder of your works.
>
> (Ps. 139:13–14 JB)

For twelve years this unnamed woman was not only ill and weak, but was also socially and religiously isolated. She seems to have been on her own. No man spoke up for her. Had she been divorced because of her ailment? So conditioned was she that she acted in secret and when discovered came forward in fear and trembling. Yet she had not been passive. Unlike the woman who was bent double and the man with the withered right hand this woman had initiated her own cure and Jesus commended her for her courage and faith. According to Jesus her faith had been the source of her healing. Through faith she had tapped into the power of Jesus and between them a miracle took place.

The behaviour of Jesus in this encounter with an unknown woman should free all Christian women from any sense of shame they may have acquired as a result of cultural and religious attitudes towards their bodily functions. Later it was made known to Peter that nothing God has created was to be considered unclean (see Acts 10:15). Commenting on this point Teresa Okure holds that, 'There is no "reign of God" where people are considered unclean or are not enabled to live fully.'[2]

POSITIVE THINKING

The woman with the haemorrhage had reason to be discouraged. Her money was gone and she was left with a long-term ailment that obliged her to live apart from people. Yet she valued herself. She spent money on her health, and risked acting contrary to her cultural regulations by joining a crowd to hear Jesus preach and by touching his garment. Jesus told her it was her faith that made her whole. And for Jesus faith casts out fear and implies taking risks. Remember when the disciples panicked during a storm on the Sea of Galilee and Jesus asked, 'Why are you afraid? Have you no faith?' (Mk 4:40 RSV)?

There will be times when each one of us has reason to be discouraged, often by circumstances beyond our control. During such times it is important to remember that there is one area over which we continue to retain personal control. It is the area of response; here there is always a choice. The response may be negative and so contribute to the destruction of self. Or after the first impulse of fear, frustration and self-pity, it is possible to respond positively and so emerge from the experience enriched rather than mentally battered. The mind is a powerful force and through cultivating positive attitudes one's sense of well-being is heightened. Negative attitudes can induce bodily ills. Women are making a new effort to touch Jesus, to connect and co-operate with his healing power and in so doing are prepared to be singled out from the crowd. Teresa Okure encouraged the same positive attitude when she wrote:

> Today, we are not to be satisfied simply with being healed. We are to join the disciples in being healers, in proclaiming that the reign of God has come, that we have touched that reign, become part of it, and have been empowered by God to become its heralds. We are in a unique position to help effect this wholeness of ourselves and of society, because like the woman with the flow of blood we have borne the weight of the illness, the alienation in society, and so should know better where it hurts and how it is to be healed.[3]

LISTENING TO THE BODY

All our information comes through the body's senses – sight, hearing, touch, taste and smell. Our ideas, experiences of well-being, delight, pain, anger, love and spirituality come through the body. Through it we hear music, feel the rhythms of dance, see landscapes, speak, walk, participate in sport, read, write, produce works of art and engineering feats. The body tells us when to eat, sleep and exercise, but many people have lost touch with its signals and force it to abide by the clock instead. The body is forever changing, bringing us new experiences as it progresses through infancy, childhood, youth, maturity and ongoing ageing.

The body is our vehicle through life. It is our last possession and when we part with it, life as we know it is over. Yet many people take the body for granted, neglect it, fail to listen to its needs. The body never lies and to push it beyond its capacity is to do violence to oneself. Depending on the care one takes of this vehicle our embodied passage through life may go smoothly or suffer a number of breakdowns. Watch how a person takes care of a motor-bike, the constant washing, oiling, fuelling, running repairs, seeing that the tyres, brakes and engine are kept in good working order. The same care is given by many to their cars. They listen to the hum of the engine, the slightest alteration or rattle is investigated for fear of an accident. Yet the same drivers may have ignored several heart-attack warnings and could endanger life if one day they slump over the steering wheel.

It is important to grasp the fact that the body is a temporary possession, that we are mortal. This should not be a morbid thought, but a stimulating reality that gives a true perspective to our whole lives. Our life-span on this earth is limited. We are in a particular time capsule shared with others. So at this moment we are sharing not only a planet but a period of time with those called into being at present. When we focus on this fact we realise that our time ration is too precious to squander on petty animosities or envies, on accumulating unnecessary things, on being bored. Instead we are stimulated to reassess our values and aims, to prioritise our relationships and to decide to welcome with a sense of joy and excitement the time remaining to us. To a Buddhist the great sin is to have been given time and space in this world and not to have learned how best to use them. The people among whom I lived in Nigeria celebrated the death of an older person. 'The ripe fruit has fallen,' they said, 'the cycle of nature is completed.' They found it difficult to accept the death of a young person. However, the reality is that some do die young and Jesus warned us that we do not know the hour or the day. Our call is to be fully alive during the time given to us.

It is through the body that we relate to others and to the world around us. For most people the body is so constructed that it is capable of intimate relationships across the sex divide. While acknowledging this fact, let us not forget there are those who were also 'knit together' in their mother's womb as hermaphrodites, combining the characteristics of both sexes, or with physical limitations that do not allow for sexual intimacy. They too are part of God's 'mysteries' to be acknowledged and appreciated. Our bodies also provide the genes and material for the next generation. It is in carrying out this function that women can become more aware of human embodiment. For many there is the experience of pregnancy and the suckling at the breast. But almost all women experience decades of monthly blood shedding, reminding them that they are capable of bearing new life. Here again the body is sending out messages. Perhaps this bodily reminder should prompt women to consider first how they might enhance their own well-being and thus be more fit to bring new life either to the next generation or on a more spiritual level to those around them.

In their effort to achieve a new sense of spiritual and bodily wholeness women are turning to God as Mother. Reflecting on the experience of Asian women Chung Hyun Kyung writes:

> God as mother and woman challenges the old concept which emphasised, along with other attributes, God as immutable and unchangeable. Woman's body grows and changes radically through menstruation and pregnancy compared to the male body. God as mother is more approachable and personable. When Asian women begin to imagine God as woman and mother, they also begin to accept their own bodies and their own womanhood in its fullness.[4]

Many Christian women are becoming more and more aware of a growing need for ritual in their lives; that is, for sacred celebratory moments in which to mark special events, especially transitional periods. Puberty is one such occasion when a young person is entrusted with the power to pass on life. Some cultures have very elaborate rituals for this transition, and as a life-carrier the young teenager is accepted into adult circles and given responsibilities within the community. The onset of the menopause is another time that also calls for a celebratory ritual, and a sacred moment in which to bless the woman and send her on her way into a new enhanced phase of life in which with her wisdom, experience and talents she can tap into a wider area of influence.

A SIMPLE LIFESTYLE

While women are gaining a new sense of personal well-being, they are also becoming aware of the fact that all is not right among humankind as a whole. Every day they hear of men, women and children dying of famine, of more and more people made redundant and deprived of an adequate income.

This message was reinforced when Jesus spoke about possessions. God knows our needs and provides sufficient for all. The first disciples realised this and pooled their resources so that all had their needs met. Their dependence on God was expressed through their dependence on the community into which they contributed their share. Preoccupation with possessions and the storing up of security for the future was seen by Jesus as sheer foolishness. To illustrate his point of view he told the story of the rich landowner who had had a bumper crop and decided to build larger barns in order to provide for many years to come. His concerns were futile as he died that night (see Lk. 12:13–21). Jesus insisted that it is wiser to find our security in heaven, and that heaven is among us.

All the great spiritual leaders from Buddha down through the centuries taught that to focus on the accumulation of wealth was to fail to understand the true object of life. I am told that G. K. Chesterton once said, 'There are two ways to get enough: one is to continue to accumulate more and more, the other is to desire less', and that George McDonald declared, 'To have what we want is riches, to be able to do without is power.' Knowing what one can do without, frees one from the tyranny of possessions and the pressures of advertising.

It is a duty of government to aim at achieving material prosperity for all. But our Western culture dictates that there should be no limits set to our rising standard of living, despite the fact that there are limits to the earth's resources. Those consuming more than their share not only harm themselves but deprive others. It has been pointed out that though the second helping you refuse may not benefit another, it will benefit you. Many Westerners eat far more than is good for them and then pay for slimming aids, or use the car to save time and then buy apparatus with which to exercise in the time saved. Our good health and sense of well-being is adversely affected by any irresponsible use of our resources.

In his book *No More Plastic Jesus,* A. D. Finnerty describes graphically the present injustice between the rich and poor. He writes as follows:

> A far more realistic image of our embattled planet might be that of an ocean liner, rather than a life-boat. This ocean liner, too, is in danger of sinking, but not so much because of the hordes of hungry passengers clinging to the rail and massed together in its dirty and dangerous holds as because of the deportment of the first-class passengers. These passengers making up 28% of the ship's list, have insisted on bringing along their automobiles, their freezers, their television sets, their kitchen disposal units, and their pets. A number of the ship's holds are filled with empty cans, bottles, discarded plastic, old newspapers and broken appliances – all the residue of first-class consumption. In other sections there are cattle, which are periodically slaughtered to provide meat for the first-class passengers, and in still other compartments there is grain to feed the cattle. On the deck of the ship are amassed assorted tanks, airplanes, explosives, and a small army of guards, which the first-class passengers have brought along in order to assure themselves of a safe and undisturbed voyage.
>
> To complete the picture we should note that the privileged passengers have some dangerous personal habits. They flush garbage down the toilets, blow tobacco smoke and shoot aerosol sprays into the ventilating system, and insist on unlimited use of the ship's limited electricity and water. Every once in a while they have a major brawl among themselves and threaten to sink the ship entirely. The ship has no captain, since the first-class passengers are afraid to give anyone authority to steer a new course or to change the ship's arrangements. Rather, there is a committee, which has no power and is not allowed access to the bridge, but permitted only to discuss possible future directions and make suggestions.[5]

To speak of the problem of the poor is misleading, for it is the rich who cause the problems. We feel compassion for those forced to live in refugee camps, yet fail to recognise that we too are being dehumanised by a consumer culture that manipulates our needs and lifestyle. In illustrating this point the Indian Jesuit Anthony de Mello described an encounter between a rich industrialist from the North and a Southern fisherman who was resting beside his boat. The industrialist asked why the man was not out fishing. The fisherman explained that he had caught sufficient fish for the day and saw no reason to go out for a second catch. The Northerner pointed out that the extra catch would mean more money with which he could buy a motor for his boat. Then with the accumulating profits a second boat could be bought and so on until he had a fleet and became as rich as the industrialist. On asking what he was to do then, the industrialist told him he could take time off to sit down and enjoy life. 'What do you think I am doing right now?' asked the fisherman.[6]

THE SIMPLE LIFESTYLE MOVEMENT

I first heard of the Simple Lifestyle Movement in 1982 when I attended a conference held in Whalley Abbey, Lancashire, England. One of the main speakers was Horace Dammers, then Dean of Bristol Cathedral. Later from his office I gained further information and learned that some people in Australia, Europe and North America felt a strong desire to win back for themselves a conscious control over their lifestyle. From these beginnings the Simple Lifestyle Movement developed. It is not an organisation but a movement that has now spread to many countries around the world. The hope is that as it grows it will bring about structural change in society so as to allow for a more just distribution of the earth's resources.

Members of the Simple Lifestyle Movement claim that the fruit of this lifestyle is a great joyousness of spirit. They warn against meanness or imposing on others, but rather encourage a willingness to share by practising a simple hospitality that enables one to invite more guests. They stress the importance of a non-judgmental attitude towards others. One of their catchphrases is, 'Question your own lifestyle, not your neighbour's.'

Compassion, self-restraint, co-operation, and celebration are the ingredients of this lifestyle, and by living it one learns that there are alternatives to living in an alienating, materialistic and competitive world. They also recognise that as intelligent beings on this planet we have a responsibility to explore the wonders of creation and to appreciate the discoveries made through modern technology. Those thinking of joining the movement are advised not to ask,

'What should I give up?' but rather, 'What do I need for a full human life?'

Living a simple lifestyle without being in some way politically involved would prove ineffectual in bringing about social change. It is important therefore to develop a global awareness as environmental and poverty issues are distorted if seen only from a local perspective. Members of the Simple Lifestyle Movement actively support economic policies that conserve and develop the earth's resources for the benefit of all. They also join other organisations that are working for a more just world society.

Asked why they have reorganised their lifestyle, members explain that it is:

1. as an act of celebration which allows for time to reflect and to enjoy more leisure with others;
2. as an act of provocation which arouses awareness of our over-consumption and unjust distribution of resources;
3. as an act of anticipation of the time when the self-confidence of the marginalised will bring about new power relationships of co-operation;
4. as an act of advocacy, giving voice to the voiceless, in bringing about a new legislated world economic order. Through living this lifestyle they experience a great sense of personal integrity.

The Simple Lifestyle Movement offers guidelines, not rules. It recommends a plan for gradual change, beginning first with a look at luxury or prestige objects and undertakings and deciding on which to let go and which to keep. The second step is to examine one's work habits and to temper them to provide for one's needs, not for the compulsive accumulation of profit. The third step is to consider how best one can make one's home a place of welcome and organise one's time so as to allow more space for reflection, leisure pursuits and social action. A simple lifestyle is not intended to be austere and colourless but rather to be free of clutter and useless anxieties. Those practising it regularly update their needs and set aside time and money for celebration and personal interests.

Some people actually sign a formal simple lifestyle commitment and meet with others so committed for mutual support in living contrary to popular expectations. The details of the commitment vary from group to group but usually include a promise not to eat or drink to excess; to take sufficient sleep for health and good temper; to be generous without being extravagant; to avoid using products that involve the exploitation of the poor; to set aside time for reflection, for leisure and for celebration with others; to be caring of those close to one, especially any person towards whom one may have a special obligation.

For Christians and all believers the Simple Lifestyle Movement includes acknowledging all creation as God's gift to us and our call to responsible stewardship. The time set aside for reflection includes prayer and study of the faith. Christians promise to work for change in the church through the power of the Spirit so that Christ's mission to bring about a reign of justice, peace and unity may be fulfilled.

PAUSE FOR REFLECTION

Luke has preserved for us the encounter between Jesus and Zacchaeus the tax-collector who lived in Jericho. One day when Jesus was in the town, Zacchaeus, because he was short in stature, climbed into a sycamore tree in order to see Jesus. As he passed by, Jesus looked up, saw Zacchaeus and called to him, asking to stay in his house. Many in the crowd grumbled because Jesus had chosen to lodge with a 'sinner'. But Zacchaeus was delighted and declared that from now on he would share half of his possessions with the poor and repay four-fold any whom he had cheated. Then Jesus told Zacchaeus that salvation had come to him that day (see Lk. 19:1–10).

Explain what you consider Jesus meant when he spoke of 'salvation'.

How do you think this 'coming of salvation' affected Zacchaeus' lifestyle during the remainder of his days on earth?

Which aspect of living simply and justly holds the most attraction for you?

Which aspect would hold the greatest unease for you?

EXERCISE 1

List occasions that you think would benefit from an appropriate ritual celebration. Decide on someone you will ask to help you plan a ritual for the next such occasion.

EXERCISE 2

Recall an unpleasant situation you were in. It might be a family argument, an interview, an occasion when you felt used, or something much worse. How did it affect your body? How did you respond?

Imagine that situation again. But this time watch yourself respond in the way you now feel is right for you.

EXERCISE 3

Sit back and relax each muscle of your body from head to toe. Close your eyes and think of each body part from the scalp, brain, eyes, down to the heart, liver, knees and on to the feet including each organ and joint on the way.

Now list what for you are the ten most important parts of your body.

Look at the list until one item keeps drawing your attention; then focus on it.

Sit back and listen to that organ or body part and recall how you have treated it. Dialogue with it, explain why you gave it the kind of treatment that you did, whether this treatment was good, bad or indifferent.

Resolve together how you will behave towards it in future.[7]

EXERCISE 4

Consider the phrase 'need, not greed'.

List what you consider to be the two most effective lifestyle changes that could be made in Western society so as to bring greater benefit to all.

Think back over the history of your country and answer the following questions:

Who was there 1,000 years ago?

Who was there 100 years ago?

Who will be there in 100 years hence?

How best can responsible stewardship be practised while still enjoying the present resources of the country?

Describe an action you could take that would enable you to be less greedy and more joyful!

GOSPEL REFLECTION
Read the story of the woman who was healed (Mk 5:24–34).

Sit back for a moment and enter into this Gospel scene.

Watch the woman standing well away from the crowd listening to Jesus.

Sense the hope rising in her as she plans to approach Jesus discreetly some time later when an opportunity offers.

Suddenly he is coming towards her and with quick thinking she manages unnoticed to touch his garment.

As she goes forward to confess, feel within you her mixed emotions, her fear of the crowd, her trust in Jesus.

Then hear Jesus say as he turns to look at you: 'Courage, your faith has made you whole.'

Stay with this moment in the presence of the Christ.

Ask to have your mind cleared of any negative thoughts towards yourself or others.

Now read slowly from Psalm 139:13–14.

Thank God for the mystery of life, of all creation, and for the wonder that is you.

If you have any particular physical problems or mental worries focus on them for a moment; then make your own prayer of trust to the all-empowering Spirit.

CLOSING ACT
Take a card and print on it either of the two statements made by Jesus to the woman who had been bleeding for twelve long years. When printed, fix it to your mirror. Jesus said:

'COURAGE, YOUR FAITH HAS MADE YOU WHOLE' (Mt. 9:22).

'GO IN PEACE, YOU ARE FREE OF YOUR TROUBLE' (Mk 5:34).

To worship in Spirit and in truth

Examining inherited attitudes

J esus lived in an occupied country in which the underground movement of rebels known as the Zealots kept the political situation in a state of tension as they agitated for freedom and independence. But this undercover warfare between the Zealots and the Romans was not the only source of division in this small country: there was also hostility between the Jews and the Samaritans.

The Samaritans

In 721 BC the Assyrians captured the land of Samaria which lies between Galilee in the north and Judea in the south. The men were taken into slavery and the land parcelled out among the conquerors who intermarried with the remaining Samaritans. Soon afterwards hordes of lions roamed through Samaria terrifying the people. Now at that time gods were considered to be powerful only within their own lands, so the Assyrian settlers requested the return of a Samaritan priest to help appease the God of Israel and so rid Samaria of the lions. As a result of this action the Samaritans became not only a people of mixed race but also of mixed religion as they worshipped through the rituals of both Israel and Assyria.

More than a century later the people of Judea were captured by the Babylonians and taken into exile. In 538 BC they were allowed to return and on reaching home planned to rebuild the Temple in Jerusalem. The Samaritans offered to help but were repulsed by the Judeans who no longer recognised them as orthodox Jews. This led to a growing enmity between the two peoples. The Samaritans built their own temple on Mount Gerazim.

JESUS AND THE SAMARITANS

By the time of Jesus the hostility between the Samaritans and the Jews was such that when the Galileans were making their pilgrimages to Jerusalem they travelled south along the east bank of the Jordan thus avoiding the Samaritan territory. However, Jesus, true to character, made the journey through Samaria. Once, the Samaritans knowing that Jesus and his companions were on their way to the Temple in Jerusalem, refused them food and hospitality. Outraged, the brothers James and John asked if they should call down fire upon these people, to which request Jesus responded with a firm rebuke (see Lk. 9:51–55).

It is Luke also who has preserved for us the much-loved story of the good Samaritan. One day a lawyer tried to trap Jesus by asking what he should do to gain eternal life. Jesus in true rabbinical style asked another question: What do the Scriptures say? The lawyer answered, giving the two great commandments: first to love God with heart and mind, and second to love one's neighbour as oneself. Jesus agreed, but the lawyer persisted: Who is my neighbour? Jesus replied with a story.

A man travelling from Jerusalem to Jericho was attacked by robbers, stripped of all he possessed and left battered and dying by the roadside. A priest who saw the man walked past on the other side. A Levite (a member of the priestly tribe) looked at the man but continued on. However, a Samaritan, on seeing the man, was filled with compassion, poured oil on his wounds, bandaged them, lifted the victim onto his donkey, brought him to an inn and took care of him. Next day he paid the innkeeper and asked him to look after the man until he, the Samaritan, was making his return journey. Which of these, asked Jesus, was neighbour to the man? The one who showed compassion, answered the lawyer. You are right, said Jesus, go and do likewise (see Lk. 10:25–37).

To get his point across, Jesus could have named the three men Samuel, Isaac and Joshua. But no, he deliberately mentioned the priest, the Levite and the Samaritan. And it was the heretical Samaritan who acted in accordance with God's compassionate love.

On another occasion Jesus again referred to the divinely tuned mind of a Samaritan. He was on his way to Jerusalem when he met with ten lepers who called out from a distance asking for help. Jesus, following the Mosaic law, told them to go and be examined by a priest. Only a priest could pronounce them clean. Realising he was cured, one man went back and threw himself in gratitude at the feet of Jesus. He was a Samaritan. Jesus wondered why it was that only the foreigner returned to praise God (see Lk. 17:11–19).

I have often heard this incident read in church, and interpreted to mean that Jesus wants us to show gratitude to God, and to give thanks for all our blessings. Never have I been asked to recognise that some members of other faiths are often more aligned to the mind of Christ and act in a more Christ-like way than many of us who call ourselves Christians.

This championing of Samaritan spirituality was not appreciated by the religious teachers. One day when in debate with Jesus they threw it up at him, 'Were we not right in saying that you are a Samaritan and have a demon in you?' (Jn 8:48 GNB). Jesus finds himself again in trouble with the authorities, this time for his attitude towards 'pagan' Samaritans; before, it was for his attitude towards women. So what will happen if Jesus meets a Samaritan woman?

THE SAMARITAN WOMAN (JN 4:1–42)
In direct contrast to the discussion with Nicodemus, a male Jewish leader who came to Jesus secretly by night (see Jn 3:1–21), John recounts at much greater length the dialogue that Jesus himself initiated with a Samaritan woman at noontime and in a public place.

On his way back to Galilee Jesus took the route through Samaria. Drawing near a Samaritan city called Sychar, Jesus sat down wearily by the well of Jacob while the disciples went on into the town to buy food. A local woman came to draw water and Jesus asked for a drink. Astonished, the woman asked the stranger why a Jew would ask a Samaritan for water. Jews did not eat or drink from the utensils of foreigners. Jesus told her that if she knew who he was she would ask him to give her the water that leads to eternal life. Interested, she asked for such water. Jesus told her to go first and call her husband. But she had no husband. Jesus agreed saying she had had five husbands and that the man she now lived with was not her husband. Immediately she perceived that here was a prophet. Changing the subject she explained that her ancestors had worshipped on the mountain nearby but that the Jews worshipped in Jerusalem. She wanted to know where God wished to be worshipped. Then Jesus declared,

> Believe me, woman, a time is coming when you will worship the Father neither on this mountain nor in Jerusalem . . . a

> time is coming and has now come when the true worshippers
> will worship the Father in spirit and truth, for they are the
> kind of worshippers the Father seeks. (Jn 4:21, 23 NIV)

Just then the disciples returned and were surprised to find Jesus
conversing with a woman, but none of them dared enquire what he
wanted of her. Then the woman left her water pot, went back to the
town and spoke of Jesus, asking if he could be the Messiah. When
the disciples offered him food, Jesus informed them that he had
food they knew nothing about. The disciples presumed someone
had brought food while they were away. Then Jesus explained that
his food was to complete the mission with which he had been
entrusted. He spoke of sowing and of reaping a harvest sown by
others.

Meanwhile, many Samaritans listened to the woman and came
out to meet Jesus. He agreed to remain two days with them.
Towards the end of his stay, the people told the woman that they
had at first believed on her word, but now they believed on the
word of Jesus.

Commentators tend to presume the woman was a 'sinner'. But
if you read the text you will see that at no point does Jesus
condemn the woman, nor does he tell her 'to sin no more' or that
her sins are forgiven. He simply mentions her home circumstances.
Could she have been a subject of the levirate law (see Deut.
25:5–10). This law laid down that it was a man's duty to marry his
brother's widow and bring up children in the dead man's name.
Was she now living under the protection of her father-in-law or
some other male member of the family?

Note that Jesus taught women personally and listened to what
they had to say. He had told Nicodemus it was necessary to be born
again in the Spirit. Now using the symbol of life-giving water Jesus
leads this woman to understand that she has within her a well of
divine activity that is the source of her wholeness. When she asked
where God should be worshipped Jesus took time to give her a full
explanation. As Teresa Okure has commented, it was to be neither
in Jerusalem nor on Gerazim, neither from the fathers nor from
tradition, but with the Spirit at work among us. She said that Jesus
was giving new birth to this Samaritan woman and for this to
happen the waters had to break.[1]

While many see the Samaritan woman as a sexual sinner, Jesus
saw her as a potential disciple and co-worker. True discipleship
begets a desire to share with others.

Just as Mary of Bethany broke womanly tradition to join herself as a disciple to Jesus, even more did the woman from Samaria violate conventions (and Jesus with her), speaking to and learning, in a public place, from a Jewish man. The Samaritan woman was led to the brink of perceiving that Jesus is the Christ, Messiah and shared this with others.[2]

She 'left her water jar'. This is a Gospel phrase comparable with they 'left their fishing nets'. Whatever her standing in the community, the Samaritans accepted this woman's witness. We will see that this was not the experience of Mary Magdalene, Joanna and Mary the mother of James who met with rejection when they reported their experience at the tomb. The Samaritan woman is a model for all missionaries. Like John the Baptist, once she had directed the people to Jesus she faded into the background. When at the Last Supper Jesus prayed for those who believe in him through the witness of others, did he remember her? She had sown the seed that others would reap. When after Pentecost the community in Jerusalem was persecuted, some fled to Samaria, where the people received them and accepted their preaching. The old antagonism seems to have been healed.

When the disciples found Jesus talking to the woman at Jacob's Well, they were astonished but did not question him. Reflecting on this point Mercy Oduyoye writes: 'They were silent. The great silence of church men over the relationship between Jesus and women, women and the Gospel, women and theology, women and the church had begun. They said nothing!'[3] At times, committed Christian women looking at the church today wonder how its leadership could have moved so far from the attitude of Jesus towards women. Disillusioned they ask with the Samaritan woman, 'Could this be the Christ?' (Jn 4:29 NIV). Teresa Okure points out that Jesus is a bringer of hope, of good news. When Christianity is bad news for women then the catechesis has to be questioned.[4]

Jesus accepted people into discipleship as they were, man or woman, Jew or Samaritan; their sex, their race, their past was not a hindrance. Always Jesus offers a future. In travelling through Samaria, in making himself known to this woman and in staying two days in Sychar, Jesus helped his disciples to overcome their people's prejudice towards the Samaritans.

CULTURAL PREJUDICE
Jesus, born and bred a Galilean Jew, had at times to question

cultural prejudices in relation to his own behaviour. He succeeded in freeing himself from the inherited attitude of his people towards their neighbours, the Samaritans, so much so that he himself was scornfully called 'a Samaritan'.

Cultural prejudices are inherited. Most of us are unaware that we entertain such prejudice. As we grew up, we presumed that our own culture is the norm and that others are strange, exotic, inferior or superior, even frightening. We have to come to realise for ourselves that others may perceive us in the same way as odd and incomprehensible. Our cultures encapsulate us and qualify everything we learn from the moment of birth. Culture is not just a collection of outward customs of dress, music or food, but is the commonly-held beliefs and attitudes which form a people's behaviour. An African child reared by Eskimos in the Arctic will think and behave like an Eskimo. Today with the communication network encircling the earth, cultures are constantly overlapping and intermixing. While helping towards mutual understanding, this may at the same time prevent us from recognising more readily our inherited prejudices.

Prejudice means to pre-judge, to form a negative evaluation based on a faulty generalisation, often of people whom we have never met. Prejudice distorts all that we see and hear. Every culture has its good and bad qualities acquired through changing circumstances. It is only when we learn to look objectively at our own culture and see ourselves as others see us that we can be freed from regarding our culture as the norm and so learn to understand and appreciate other cultures.

THINKING AND ACTING FROM WITHIN ROLES

Another area that can lead to misunderstanding and prejudice is that of the roles we fill throughout life. We are relating to others not only from within our culture but also from within the role we are filling at that moment; for example, daughter/mother, shopper/salesperson, doctor/patient, etc. How we perceive the other will depend on how well we are managing our respective roles. Sometimes we make a general judgment of others, forgetting that we are meeting them within the limitations of their immediate role. I remember a bus driver who was often irritable with the passengers. One day the woman sitting next to me said, 'I pity the wife that has to live with him.' The fact that he seemed unsuitable for the role in which we met him, and was unable to handle the vagaries of the public, did not prove he was tensed up at home. He may have been a companionable husband who found gardening very relaxing.

Pause, and consider for a moment your own responses with regard to roles. If you fail in a role, either in a relationship or a job, do you write yourself off as a failure? Or do you think, 'I have failed as a daughter', or 'I have not the personality for a management position'? Some people feel totally useless because of an inadequacy in one particular area. And, of course, they judge others in the same way. This is especially damaging if that other is a child.

Note that most of our roles are temporary; we grow out of some, change, and take on others. Look again at the roles you enjoy. Can you make more time for them? Look at the roles you find burdensome. Can you drop any of them or gradually work your way out of them? Do you want to start working at the roles you neglect at present? Decide to be positive about any role you cannot at present drop. Be in control of your attitudes.

The roles through which we relate to others will influence our perception of the other. For example, Ronan will be known quite differently by his mother, brother, wife, son, niece, employer, neighbour, friend, competitor, client, religious minister, and so on. Once we become aware that we are encountering others across the confines of cultures and roles we can begin to recognise our subconscious prejudices.

Depending on attitudes acquired in the family and school we may stereotype people of different races, nations, religions, professions, class, political parties, etc. We can even stereotype animals. In fact our parents or guardians passed on not only their own responses but those of their parents and guardians before them, so that each one of us is left carrying the prejudices of at least three generations. Another source of prejudice can come from our previous experiences. If we have had a good or bad experience with a nurse or a German it may leave us either accepting or critical of the nurses and Germans we meet in future. Sometimes a person may subconsciously remind us of a person we did not like and so we remain reserved with the newcomer. Yet all they may have in common is a hairstyle, a mannerism or an accent. Note, we all speak with an accent. Whatever the source of the prejudice it prevents us from being open to the individuality of the person.

Often our prejudices lead us to judge others negatively because of qualities which we consider positive in ourselves! For example, a person who values hard work, discipline, ambition, financial independence, success, when she meets these qualities in another person may declare that the other person is a workaholic, hardhearted, dominating, indifferent to the needs of others and puts self first. Yet it is amazing how a prejudice disappears when the focus of it is encountered personally within the family. An interracial, international or inter-faith marriage can alter our views. When a family member enters a cult, reveals he or she is homosexual, gets divorced, or is accused of petty crime we can reach new depths of compassion and understanding. The good news preached by Jesus is that each of us is generated by the same divine power, that we are one in Christ, branches of the same vine, and carry within us the same divine life that is our salvation. The difficulty lies in accepting the obvious conclusion that we are all one family, sisters and brothers to each other.

Jesus made some hard statements in order to get this message across. Once, some scribes from Jerusalem followed Jesus north and accused him of being possessed by Beelzebul. When they heard what had been said of him, his mother and brothers went looking for him in order to take him home. They arrived at the house in which he was teaching and sent for him. On being told that his mother, his brothers and sisters were outside asking for him, Jesus looked at the people listening to him and told them that they were his mother and his brothers: for whoever observes the will of God is his brother, sister and mother (see Mk 3:20–35). These are strong words in the circumstances, but they were used by Jesus to get across the difficult message that is basic to all Christian living.

Jesus' call to conversion includes renouncing our prejudices. The compassion and understanding expected between sisters and brothers are to be extended to all whom we encounter. In his dealings with the Samaritans, Jesus has shown us how it is done. His first approach to the woman was to ask for her help. Then in the conversation that followed he gave her the good news, that the Spirit of God dwelt within her, empowering her. Obviously she was a woman of faith; and thus strengthened, her first thought was to share the good news with her people. Then, when Jesus saw the good will of the people he stayed awhile with them. There was no question here of shaking the dust of their town from his sandals.

PAUSE FOR REFLECTION
The story of Jesus' encounter with the Samaritan woman

challenges us to reflect on roles, attitudes and prejudices in our own lives.

Try to identify some of your own prejudices; that is, your negative attitudes towards certain types of individuals or groups which are based on inherited assumptions rather than personal knowledge and facts. You may be prejudiced against some races, nationalities, religions, social classes, medical practices, forms of music, acquaintances, and so on.

Try to recall three negative attitudes that you now recognise are inherited.

Can you recognise a prejudice that you acquired personally by generalising from an individual you met or some experience you had.

Name to yourself any prejudices you intend to offload.

EXERCISE 1

Take a sheet of paper and list down the numbers 1 to 36. Now read the list of roles you might fill in life and add any others relevant to you.

1. Infant	2. Schoolchild	3. Grandchild
4. Son/daughter	5. Sister/brother	6. Niece/nephew
7. Cousin	8. Student	9. Worker/unemployed
10. Leader	11. Spouse	12. Parent
13. Neighbour	14. Friend	15. Uncle/aunt
16. Grandparent	17. Church member	18. Carer
19. Patient	20. Visitor	21. Club member
22. Tourist	23. Competitor	24. Lobbyist
25. Job-seeker	26. Sportsperson	27. Client/customer
28. Invalid	29. Widow/er	30. Pensioner
31. Priest	32. Religious	33.
34.	35.	36.

On your sheet of paper:

Line through the number of any role you once filled but now no longer fill.

Circle the roles you fill at present.

Bracket the number of any role that may await you in the future.

Star the roles you enjoy.

Cross the roles you find burdensome.

Put a question mark by the roles you now fill but do not give time to.

Now let's get away from the present reality and start daydreaming:

Write down three roles you would like to fill in the future.

Write down the first three preparatory steps you need to take in order to make your dream come true. It might be to start saving, or studying, or rearranging your time, or finding another person with a similar desire, etc.

It is up to ourselves to turn our dreams into realities.

EXERCISE 2

Take another sheet of paper and list numbers 1 to 30. Then read down the following list of people and quickly write beside the corresponding number on your paper the first word that comes to mind. Speed is of the essence in this exercise. Give yourself no time to edit what your write.

1. US politician	16. Missionary
2. Peasant activist	17. Moslem
3. Environmentalist	18. Nun
4. British royal	19. Fundamentalist Christian
5. Communist ruler	20. Orthodox Jew
6. Homosexual	21. Drug baron
7. Unmarried mother	22. Oil billionaire
8. Feminist	23. Long-term unemployed person
9. Criminal gang member	24. Aid worker
10. Arab woman	25. Farmer
11. South African white	26. AIDS patient
12. Serb	27. OAP invalid
13. Aborigine	28. Mentally retarded child
14. Russian	29. Plastic surgeon
15. Japanese	30. Arms manufacturer

Read over your words and mark with an X any words you consider as stereotyping, either good or bad, of the person concerned.

If you have stereotyped any person, try to recall from where or from whom this attitude came.

Is there any person on the list with whom you would feel a reluctance to sit down and listen to his or her problems? If there is, ask yourself 'Why?' Place a star against the relevant numbers.

How many of your negative responses came from preconceived ideas and ignorance? How many are the result of personal knowledge?

Note in which section you were most negative: political, religious, social, racial, medical.

What have you learned about yourself from this exercise?

EXERCISE 3

Sit back for a moment and imagine that you have mysteriously changed into a member of another race and class.

Get in touch with your new feelings.

How do you now perceive your own people and class?

In your mind join your family, then a group of friends. How do they respond to this new stranger in their midst? How do you experience their reactions?

How are you treated when you go to your local shops, pub, church, etc? (Take ten minutes or so entering into this experience.)

What have you learned about your local people?

What have you learned about yourself?

GOSPEL REFLECTION

Sit comfortably, and quietly set yourself in the scene by the well. Watch the woman approach and Jesus initiating a conversation. Become aware of the dynamism present between the two as the relationship develops.

Take time to think over the important answer Jesus gave to her question about worship. He explained to her that the place of worship is not of primary importance, but rather that true worship must be offered through the Spirit and in truth.

As the disciples return, notice the woman slipping away and later see her returning with some of the townspeople.

As Jesus gets up to go with the people he turns and asks you:

'. . . . . (name), how and where do you worship?'

'I . . . .
. . . .'

Then Jesus probes further: 'How would you explain or witness to the Good News among your people?'

Thinking for a while, you answer, 'I . . . .
. . . .'

Finally, looking at you intently, Jesus asks, 'Is there anything you would leave behind?'

Again thinking a while you reply, 'I . . . .
. . . .'

CLOSING PRAYER
Remain quietly in the presence of the divine mystery allowing the Spirit to lead you in prayer.

6

THE TRUTH WILL MAKE YOU FREE

UNDERSTANDING ASSERTIVENESS

In his encounter with the Samaritan woman by the well in Sychar, we saw the openness of Jesus towards his half Jewish, half Gentile compatriots who shared with him a knowledge of the Bible and who awaited the coming of a Messiah. Now we travel with Jesus outside his country and watch him as he dialogues with a Gentile woman.

JESUS AND THE GENTILE WOMAN (MK 7:24–30, MT. 15:21–28)
There are two accounts of this incident. In Mark (the earlier account), Jesus had gone north near to the region of Tyre on the Phoenician coast. There he stayed privately in a house 'and did not want anyone to know it' (Mk 7:24 NIV). A woman, whose little daughter was seriously ill, heard of Jesus and, entering the house, fell at his feet. She asked that her little girl be cured. Jesus told her that the children of the house had to be fed first, meaning the people of Israel. Then he added that it was not right to throw their bread to the dogs. She was not cowered by his response but pointed out that even the dogs ate the bread that fell from the children's table. Impressed by her spirit and tenacity, Jesus assured the woman that her daughter was cured.

According to Matthew the encounter took place in the street. The woman called out to Jesus pleading on behalf of her daughter who was possessed. Jesus ignored her and the disciples urged him to send her away as she continued shouting after them. Finally Jesus said to her that he was sent only to the lost sheep of the house of Israel. She came forward and kneeling before him asked for his help. Jesus insisted that it was not right to take the children's bread and throw it to the dogs. She agreed but added that even the dogs fed on the crumbs dropped beneath the children's table. Then Jesus answered her, 'Woman, you have great faith' (Mt. 15:28 NIV). From that moment her daughter was cured.

'Possession' (as has been explained in Chapter 3), often referred to mental illness. Was the 'little daughter' as described by Mark epileptic, hyperactive, disturbed or just a difficult child? Many parents could relate to this woman's anxiety and to her concern for her child.

'Dog' was a derogatory term used in reference to the Gentiles.

'Bread' as used by Jesus at times meant teachings. One day when the disciples were out with Jesus it was discovered that they had forgotten to bring bread. Later Jesus warned them against the bread of the Pharisees and Sadducees. The disciples thought he was reminding them of their neglect in not providing food for the journey. He rebuked them, asking had they already forgotten the feeding of the five thousand. Then they understood that he was referring not to food but to the teachings of the Pharisees and Sadducees (see Mt. 16:5–12).

In his encounter with the Gentile woman is Jesus telling her that his ministry is restricted to the people of Israel? Social mores forbade her to approach a man in public, but obviously she had no man to speak up for the girl. So with the courage of faith she risked acting contrary to cultural expectations. Using no intermediary she went straight to Jesus, she entered the house, she called out to him in the street. She trusted herself to plead her cause and she trusted in the goodness of the other. Her assertiveness was the measure of her concern.

Jesus did not initiate this encounter. It was the woman who sought out Jesus and despite the antagonism of the disciples and the fact that Jesus ignored her at first, she persisted until she got a hearing. Jesus behaved quite differently when asked by Jairus to heal his twelve-year-old daughter, then he set off with him immediately. Again when the Roman officer asked that his servant be healed, Jesus offered to go with him.

However, in this Gentile woman, Jesus had met his match. Even his harsh response did not deflect her. Apart from his mother at Cana, this woman is the only person on record to have outwitted Jesus in an argument. He recognised her faith and realised that together they could work miracles. Did he at that moment remember his own rejection in his home town of Nazareth? 'He could not do any miracles there. . . . And he was amazed at their lack of faith' (Mk 6:5–6 NIV).

This encounter is important to the whole Gentile ministry. Had Jesus believed that he was sent only to those of faith and that faith was to be found only among the people of the covenant? Before he met this woman, Jesus, when sending out the twelve, had told them to avoid Gentile territory and Samaritan towns, and to go only to the children of Israel (see Mt. 10:5–6). He was constantly surprised at finding faith among the Gentiles. When the Roman officer pointed out to him that as a Jew he was forbidden to enter a Gentile house and that it would be sufficient for him to say but the word, Jesus 'was astonished and said to those following him, "I tell you the truth, I have not found anyone in Israel with such great faith" ' (Mt. 8:10 NIV). Was this attitude a Jewish prejudice that Jesus had to overcome? And was it through the Gentile woman that he came to realise that the Spirit is not confined to any one nation or religion, that the 'reign of God' and his own mission extended to whoever responded with faith?

Whatever the answers to these questions, Jesus is a model for all missionaries. He did not belittle the religion of the Gentiles, but listened to this Syro-Phoenician woman and accepted her insights. Through his encounters with foreigners he was able to free himself from the limitations of his own culture and to continue 'to grow in wisdom'.

ASSERTIVE VERSUS AGGRESSIVE

The word 'assertive' is often understood to be another word for aggressive. This is a total misunderstanding of the meaning of assertiveness. To be assertive is to act with self-respect while at the same time respecting others, to defend one's own position without belittling another's: to exercise personal rights without infringing on the rights of others. It is to try and avoid an 'I win, you lose' situation.

The aggressive person on the other hand sets out to win at all costs, in either of two ways: overt or covert. The overt way is to try and control the other, to enhance self at the expense of others. This is done by shouting, interrupting, ridiculing, embarrassing, blaming or physically attacking the other. Another form of overt aggression can be patronising, making decisions for others without consulting them. Aggression always generates resentment. Occasionally it can be justified, for example, in a moment of danger or crisis when quick results are required.

The second form of aggression is covert. It gains its ends by remaining stubbornly silent, or by being evasive, by saying 'Yes' and acting 'No'. A regular ploy is to play helpless and so force the other to conform or feel guilty. A person who resorts to such devious behaviour can trigger bodily reactions within themselves and end up with headaches, stomach aches, high blood pressure, etc. Seduction and manipulation are other aspects of covert aggression. In most societies aggressive women are not acceptable. Men often claim not to understand women and this is not surprising as 'feminine behaviour' is in fact a series of survival tactics used by women in order to retain some control over their lives within a male-oriented culture. The small girl learns 'to wrap Daddy round her finger'. The older girl 'plays hard to get'. Such manipulative behaviour eventually works havoc with relationships between women and men.

Assertive people aim at achieving truth and honesty in all their dealings. They are equally comfortable expressing positive or negative opinions so that you always know where you stand with them. Nor do they come across as a threat, for even when the encounter is negative they leave others with their dignity intact. Assertive people take responsibility for their decisions and actions; there is no attempt at blaming people or circumstances.

For various reasons they may choose to remain passive at times, perhaps because they want to keep their job, or not upset an older friend, or simply because they are not feeling well. The important fact is that assertive people make choices and are content not to have it their way all the time. They can also choose to be aggressive if a situation calls for such a response. Sometimes they simply 'fall from grace'; however, the difference is that they know it, take responsibility for their behaviour and try to make amends.

WOMEN TAKING RESPONSIBILITY

Passive people play safe, avoid risks and try not to provoke others, with the result that they are imposed upon. They constantly fall in with what others decide for them and so lose touch with their own needs. They are often praised as selfless people, but such selfless people have no positive self-image. In fact they are self-denying, and if underneath they feel totally powerless this can lead to alcoholism and other illnesses. Such passive behaviour plays havoc with relationships between women and men. The woman without self-esteem makes constant emotional demands on those around her. Friends, colleagues and family members have to affirm her constantly with compliments and attention. Her emotional dependency makes her hard to work with or live with. The self-confident assertive woman is less demanding, has fewer false expectations of people and roles, and is capable of sustaining solid friendships.

Female passivity has nurtured male domination. Among Christian feminists today, passive and manipulative behaviour when practised to the detriment of either self or others is regarded as sinful. It is time women accepted responsibility for the way they are treated by others. If you succumb when shouted at or belittled, you will be shouted at and belittled. If your known response to flattery is to comply with another's wishes, you will be flattered. If you allow others to make decisions for you, you will go unconsulted. If you behave like a doormat you will be used as a doormat. In most encounters we are at least 50 per cent responsible for the way we are treated.

The only person you can change is yourself. It is important to remember that the practice of assertiveness does not give a licence to be forthright and outspoken at the expense of another's feelings. The assertive person is confident enough to give a little, is not rigid, and learns to practise justice with compassion. By changing your own attitudes towards self and others your behaviour becomes more self-assured, which in turn sets off a positive response in others. The quickest way to change others is to change yourself. However, the improved responses will come more gradually from those who know you, as it will take more than one encounter for them to realise they now have to deal with a new you. Those who hitherto found you aggressive will be surprised and no doubt relieved. Those who took advantage of your passivity will be disconcerted for a while. Change requires personal effort. The choice is yours. If today, for whatever reason, you decide that it is best for you to play the passive doormat role, then in justice to those around you avoid the 'martyr complex' and be a cheerful doormat!

The Gentile woman was assertive. She showed respect to Jesus but did not allow her own worth to be diminished. She kept her dignity even when the disciples tried to be rid of her. Many women in the church today report meeting with similar opposition when they seek to come closer to Jesus in his ministry of healing and sharing the bread. The Gentile woman was articulate, not awed, and could argue her point in equal debate. Jesus' response was not one of pity but of delight. He recognised her Spirit-given insights, accepted their challenge and a girl child became whole. Around the world today there are many suffering children working in sweat shops, living on the streets, abused in their homes, all waiting to be set free from society's demons and made whole. These children need assertive adults to 'call out' on their behalf, as did that Gentile woman for her suffering daughter.

SAYING 'NO' WITH A SMILE
People who have learned to become assertive are at ease when asking a favour from another. Nor are they disconcerted or blaming if the answer is 'No', for they respect the rights and reasonableness of others and do not seek to impose or manipulate. Likewise, they are themselves comfortable saying 'No' when it is not opportune to consent to another's request. They would regard it as dishonest to say 'Yes' when they really wanted to say 'No'. Experience has proved that a begrudging consent leads to future strain in a relationship. Some people say 'Yes' out of a sense of obligation or from a fear of being disliked. A person in that situation feels trapped, the stomach muscles tighten, the mouth goes dry and a general feeling of resentment comes over the person. Such people then blame the other for asking, when if anyone is to be blamed it is themselves for not having learned to say 'No' with a smile.

Learning to say 'No' is a necessary social skill. It can be done without giving offence or leaving oneself feeling guilty. It is important also to think of the other's feelings and not make the other feel guilty for asking. Most people can accept a reasonable 'No'; it is the way the refusal is given that causes the hurt.

While keeping in mind that everyone has the right to say 'No', make it clear that the 'No' is to the present request and not necessarily to future ones. It is risky to try to spare the other's feelings with an invented excuse, because if this is found out trust is broken and the hurt is all the greater. Nor is it wise to over-apologise. A simple 'Sorry' accompanied, if so wished, by a given reason is best. For example, 'No. Sorry, but I'm too tired now to give it my full attention.' Or, 'No. Sorry, that time is already planned.' Once the refusal has been made, change the subject, or bring the encounter to a close. If the topic is kept open there is the possibility of the other becoming persistent, which could lead to unpleasant results. But, if the person is persistent and nags or tries flattery, then use what is called the broken-record technique. That is, keep repeating your first refusal with a clear 'No' each time. 'No. I can't oblige this time.' Or, 'No. It's not convenient on this occasion.' If the wording is altered there is the danger of being reasoned with and being drawn into giving excuses and then the situation could become nasty. If taken by surprise, simply ask for time to think it over. In some cases it is wise to get the request repeated by asking for a clarification as to precisely what is being asked of one.

At a meeting held by the Irish Society for the Prevention of Cruelty to Children, we were told that during a recent survey 1,000 children were asked what they most wanted from their parents. The children's three top priorities were that parents would: first, listen to them; second, be kind to them; third, keep their promises.[1] Children as well as adults like to know where they stand with people. They are comfortable with a firm 'Yes' or a firm 'No'.

JESUS AND REFUSALS

In his account of the Sermon on the Mount, Matthew records Jesus as supporting this view. 'Let your word be Yes for Yes, and No for No' (Mt. 5:37 Knox).

Matthew also records Jesus as supporting a firm 'No' in the parable of the wise and foolish bridesmaids (Mt. 25:1–13). There were ten bridesmaids waiting to escort the bridegroom. Five were foolish and five were wise. The bridegroom was delayed and the ten bridesmaids, waiting with their lamps lit and ready, fell asleep. At midnight word came of the bridegroom's approach. On waking, the bridesmaids were faced with a problem. Five had brought oil with which to tend their lamps, five had not. The five foolish bridesmaids begged their companions to share their oil with them. But the five wise ones were firm and said, 'No! There will not be enough for you and for us; you had better go to the dealers and buy some for yourselves' (Mt. 25:9 NRSV).

While they were away the bridegroom came, the doors were shut and the banquet served. When the foolish late-comers returned and knocked on the door asking to be allowed to enter, they were met with yet another firm 'No'.

At the end of the story Matthew recalls the closing remarks made by Jesus. 'Keep awake therefore, for you know not the day nor the hour' (Mt. 25:13 NRSV). The parable opened with Jesus saying that the kingdom of heaven is like this. By being passive and unprepared for the responsibilities entrusted to us are we failing to promote the reign of God among us?

When this parable is discussed in women's groups temperatures tend to rise and emotions become raw. Usually it is the five foolish bridesmaids who get all the sympathy, while the five wise ones are rejected outright. Not so with Jesus. It was the responsibility of the bridesmaids to light the way ahead for the bridegroom and his companions as they came into the wedding banquet. Obviously Jesus did not approve of women falling down on this important ministry. Is his call the same to women today? 'Awake, the bridegroom is coming!'

PAUSE FOR REFLECTION

How did you respond to 'Yes' and 'No' in your childhood?

Did you get your own way by nagging, throwing a tantrum, wheedling?

If so, how does it affect your behaviour now?

What precautions do you need to take in order to keep the Christ light shining in today's world?

EXERCISE 1

List people in your family, workplace, church, etc. whom you find it hard to oppose. Now read back over your list and after each name ask yourself 'Why?' (Is it because you fear the person, are reluctant to hurt the other, feel inadequate in his or her presence, etc?).

Are there people, e.g. children, employees, nervous people, towards whom you are inclined to be aggressive? List them and ask 'Why?'

What have you learned about yourself from this exercise?

EXERCISE 2

Think of a self-confident assertive person, man or woman, whom you know. Sit back and replay in your mind an incident in which this person behaved with controlled assertiveness. What did you admire most about this person's behaviour?

Take time to imagine yourself acting assertively in the following situations: questioning your doctor, bank manager, or child's teacher during a consultation. Refusing a request without giving offence or a false excuse.

GOSPEL REFLECTION

As Jesus travelled outside his own country a Gentile woman kept calling to him to make her daughter whole. His disciples begged him to send her away. Instead Jesus stopped and explained to the woman that he was sent only to his own people, the Jews, and that it was not right to throw their bread to the dogs. She stood her ground and reminded Jesus that the dogs ate the crumbs that fell from the table. Thus challenged, Jesus declared: 'Woman, your faith is great! What you desire will be done.'

Then turning to me Jesus asked: ' . . . . (name), what challenge have you for the community of my disciples today?'

Thinking a while, I answered: ' . . . .

. . . . '

Looking at me earnestly Jesus replied: 'What faith step are you prepared to take so that together we may accomplish what you desire?'

I said: 'Jesus, ...

. . . . '

CLOSING PRAYER

Stay quietly in the divine presence for a while.

7

THE WORD BECAME HUMAN AND LIVED
AMONG US

THE MAN JESUS

When discussing Jesus, theologians sometimes refer to a high christology and a low christology. A high christology concentrates on the divine nature in Jesus and was the perspective of European classical christology. Low christology looks at the life of Jesus from the point of view of his humanity and is the form of christology emphasised in the documents of Vatican II.

I have noticed among some of us who were brought up to focus on Jesus as God, a tendency to dismiss the reality of his humanity with comments such as, 'Ah, well, he was God and knew what was going to happen.' Such an attitude undermines the whole mystery of the Incarnation and of our redemption.

We have no eye-witness biography of Jesus. The Gospels give the faith reflections of four different communities and were written by and for those who accepted Jesus as the Christ. Known locally as Jesus-bar-Joseph, it was only towards the end of his life that a few disciples began to suspect Jesus might be the long-awaited Messiah or Christ. It was not until after his death and resurrection that he was referred to as Jesus the Christ, and finally Jesus Christ. Christ is a title describing the role he fulfilled. The Johannine community stated clearly that their Gospel was written '. . . in order that you may believe that Jesus is the Messiah, the Son of God, and that through your faith in him you may have life' (Jn 20:31 GNB).

The Gospels are second generation documents which record the acts and teachings of Jesus as handed down and reflected on by those who had known Jesus in the flesh. We cannot, in fact, quote with certainty anything that Jesus ever said or did. When quoting from the Gospels it would be more accurate to say, 'The Matthean community recorded Jesus as saying . . .' or, 'The Lucan Church presented Jesus as challenging . . .' Despite the messianic focus of the Gospels it is possible while reading them to glimpse the human circumstances in which Jesus lived, and to sense the full humanity of the man.

THE NAZARENE

Jesus was born in a small country occupied by the Romans. The Roman governor resided in the Mediterranean coastal town of Caesarea. The royal family, the Herodians, were only partly Jewish and so not acceptable to the people. Herod Antipas had been educated in Rome and was now a puppet-king presiding in another Roman-built town, Tiberias, situated on the western shores of the Sea of Galilee. The Jews avoided these towns and there is no record of Jesus ever having entered them. Both the governor and the king maintained residences in Jerusalem and travelled there for the festivals. Rome recognised the high priest and his council as the religious leaders of the people.

So Jesus grew up among a conquered people in the northern province of Galilee. He never experienced what it felt like to be a free citizen. When he was about nine years of age his fellow-countryman, Simon the Galilean, led a rebellion against the Romans but was overpowered and he and his companions were crucified. The local carpenters were more than likely pressurised into producing the necessary crosses, and in the ensuing atmosphere of deep resentment the boy Jesus would have become aware of the raw feelings among his people. For the Jews saw themselves as a religious nation ruled by God through their anointed leaders; therefore to be executed by foreigners would be for many spirit-destroying.

As a young man Jesus, like Joseph, worked as a carpenter. Without the help of modern equipment it was a trade that required physical strength, and in the process of sawing and hammering, Jesus would have developed strong muscles and probably calloused hands. He would also have needed skill in negotiating a just price for his product and labour, no easy task when offering a public service in one's own village.

Jesus spent over twenty-five years of his time on earth as a manual worker, as an adult member of his family, and as a neighbour in a rural community centred around the synagogue.

JESUS, THE ORTHODOX JEW

It is recorded that Jesus normally attended synagogue on the Sabbath and that at times he was invited to read and comment on the text. When Jesus embarked upon what today we would call his second career he became an itinerant teacher and was addressed as Rabbi or Master. The Evangelists report that during his public life he preached in synagogues throughout Galilee (see Mt. 4:23, and 9:35, Mk 1:39, Lk. 4:44). The same Evangelists describe his last visit to Jerusalem to celebrate the Passover and John adds his presence in Jerusalem for the Feast of Tabernacles when he preached in the Temple. Having healed a leper Jesus directed him to go straight to the priest and to have a sacrifice offered in accordance with the law of Moses (Mt. 8:4). He is presented as conscientious in the practice of his religion and is seen teaching within its structures.

Although orthodox, Jesus had no hesitation in questioning some of the religious attitudes of his time. When his disciples were accused of breaking the Sabbath law by picking and eating grain he declared that the Sabbath was intended to serve people, not people the Sabbath. When he himself was condemned for healing a crippled man on the Sabbath he asked, 'What does our Law allow us to do on the Sabbath? To help or to harm? To save a man's life or to destroy it?' (Mk 3:4 GNB). He condemned religious leaders for putting their own laws and traditions before the law of Moses and singled out in particular the practice of corban. Quoting the commandment which said, honour your father and your mother, Jesus continued,

> But you say, Let a man tell his father or his mother, all the money out of which you might get help from me is now Corban (that is, an offering to God), and then you will not let him do any more for father or mother. With this and many like observances, you are making God's law ineffectual through the tradition you have handed down. (Mk 7:11–14 Knox)

In Judaism, theology is done through argument and disputation; therefore, when today Jewish scholars read the Gospels they recognise Jesus as one of their own and do not see him as particularly antagonistic towards the religious teachers of his time.

Matthew records two similar encounters. The first was when some Scribes and Pharisees pointed out that the disciples of Jesus did not wash their hands before eating in accordance with ritual rules. Jesus reminded them of their abuse of corban and then declared before the listening crowd that it was not unwashed hands or the food that was eaten that made one unclean, but how one behaved. Later the disciples said to Jesus, 'Do you know that the Pharisees had their feelings hurt by what you said?', to which Jesus responded, 'Don't worry about them! They are blind leaders of the blind. . . .' (Mt. 15:1–20 GNB). He then went on to explain that what made a person unclean were the evil intentions that lead to murder, adultery, robbery and slander.

While teaching in Jerusalem, during his last week on earth, Jesus was asked if it was in keeping with Jewish law to pay taxes to the Romans. He replied, 'You hypocrites! Why are you trying to trap me? Show me the coin for paying the tax!' (Mt. 22:18 GNB). On seeing the emperor's image on the coin, Jesus said they should give to Caesar what was Caesar's and to God what was God's. Later, on the same day, some Sadducees came to question Jesus on life after death and on the commandments. All were amazed at the authority with which he answered and dared to ask no more questions. However, Jesus was not finished, he accused the religious leaders of obeying the lesser laws such as setting aside a tenth of their herbs for the service of God, '. . . but you neglect to obey the really important teachings of the Law, such as justice and mercy and honesty. These you should practise, without neglecting the others. Blind guides! You strain a fly out of your drink, but swallow a camel!' (Mt. 23:23–24 GNB).

Though teaching within the structures of his religion there were times when Jesus taught in private homes away from synagogues and the Temple. And although he was conscientious about participating in public worship, Jesus also seems to have undertaken extra devotions, as when he went to the Jordan to be baptised by John or withdrew into the desert to pray.

JESUS, THE CHRIST
For almost two centuries before Jesus was born, the Jews had begun to look forward to the coming of a Messiah or Christ; that is, one anointed to lead the people and bring them salvation. Expectations varied. Some hoped for another military king like David, who would overthow the Romans and restore the monarchy. Others prayed for a new Moses, a prophet who would guide the people in the way of salvation.

The Zealots were determined to drive the Romans from the land and to set up a kingdom subject to Jewish law. Among the twelve companions chosen by Jesus was one Simon the Zealot. After the feeding of the five thousand those present wondered if Jesus was the Messiah. Seeing that they were about to take him by force and proclaim him king, Jesus escaped into the hills. Later, as he made his last entry into Jerusalem seated on a donkey, the crowd lining the streets called out, 'Blessed is the King who comes in the name of the Lord!' (Lk. 19:38 RSV). When arrested that Passover week and brought before the high priest and his council, Jesus was asked, 'Are you the Messiah, the Son of the Blessed God?' 'I am,' answered Jesus. . . .' The High Priest . . . said, 'We don't need any more witnesses! You heard his blasphemy. What is your decision?' (Mk 14:61–64 GNB). He was condemned to death.

The power to carry out the death penalty had been denied to the Jewish council. Therefore, Jesus was taken to Pilate, the governor, who was in Jerusalem for the festival. The religious charge of blasphemy would carry no weight with the Romans, so a political charge was produced. The priests brought Jesus before Pilate and said, 'We caught this man misleading our people, telling them not to pay taxes to the Emperor and claiming that he himself is the Messiah, a king' (Lk. 23:2 GNB).

Though for three years Jesus proclaimed a spiritual kingdom that called for personal repentance, some of his disciples persisted to the end in regarding him as a possible military leader. After his death two of them fled Jerusalem but the risen Christ caught up with them on the road to Emmaus. Thinking him a stranger they spoke to him about Jesus, adding, 'Our hope had been that he would be the one to set Israel free!' (Lk. 24:21 JB). The risen Christ explained the Scriptures to them, beginning with Moses and all the prophets showing how it was inevitable that the Messiah would suffer. The two disciples returned to Jerusalem to rejoin the community there and admitted to each other that they had felt their hearts burn within them as the Scriptures were interpreted. Luke also recorded that even at the moment of the ascension, some of the disciples asked, 'Lord, has the time come? Are you going to restore the Kingdom to Israel?' (Acts 1:6 JB). It seems that many of the male disciples believed that they were to be part of a new political kingdom. It took the Pentecost experience to enable them to grasp fully that the reign of God depended not on arms but on a conversion of heart, an acceptance of others as sisters and brothers.

For Jesus, messiahship had meant the more prophetic role of teacher and healer. Half a century later, when the Matthean

Church wrote its version of the Good News, Jesus was presented as the new Moses proclaiming a law of compassion and forgiveness. The Sermon on the Mount which outlines the new Christian law forms a parallel image to that of Moses imparting the older law from the foothills of Mount Sinai (see Mt. 5, 6 and 7, Ex. 19:25).

JESUS, A HUNTED AND REJECTED MAN

In the 1980s, when I reflected on the Gospels with groups in Dublin a number of the women said that if they had lived during the time of Jesus, if they had met him and been taught by him, conversion would have been so much easier. In response to this view we began to re-read the Gospels, studying the reaction Jesus inspired in those who heard him preach.

In the much-loved Johannine Gospel, written seventy years after the death and resurrection of Jesus, we found Jesus being opposed not by the Romans but by some of his own people. In chapter 1 we read, 'He came to his own home, and his own people received him not' (Jn 1:11 RSV). By chapter 5 when Jesus had healed a man who had been an invalid for thirty-eight years we are told that the religious authorities '. . . began to persecute Jesus, because he had done this healing on the Sabbath.' Jesus defended himself by saying, 'My Father is always working, and I too must work' (Jn 5:16–18 GNB). This claim decided the religious leaders that Jesus must be killed, not only because he broke the Sabbath law but because in calling God his Father he had made himself equal to God.

In John 6 we get the account of the feeding of the five thousand people who had followed Jesus when he went to the other side of the Sea of Galilee. The next day the people again went looking for Jesus and found him teaching in the synagogue of his adopted home town of Capernaum. He accused them of seeking him purely for a free meal and not for spiritual nourishment. He then went on to give his great Eucharistic discourse in which he said that he was the bread of life and that whoever ate his flesh would become one with him and live for ever. Many of those who heard him said, 'This is intolerable language. How can anyone accept it? . . . After this, many of his disciples left him and stopped going with him' (Jn 6:60, 66 JB).

During the Feast of Tabernacles Jesus did not want to go up to Jerusalem, '. . . because the Jewish authorities there were wanting to kill him' (Jn 7:1 GNB). His brothers advised him to go but Jesus told them to go on ahead, and John added, 'Not even his brothers believed in him' (Jn 7:5 GNB). Soon after this Jesus travelled secretly to the festival. 'There was much whispering about him in the crowd. "He is a good man," some people said. "No," others said, "he is misleading the people"' (Jn 7:12 GNB). When the festival was half over Jesus began to teach in the Temple and asked, '"Why are you trying to kill me?" "You have a demon in you!" the crowd answered' (Jn 7:19–20 GNB).

The chief priests sent guards to arrest Jesus but there was a division among the people, some saying he was the Messiah, others that he was a prophet, while others wanted him arrested. The guards withdrew and returned to the council elders saying no one had ever taught like this man. Scornfully the elders asked, 'Did he fool you, too?' (Jn 7:47 GNB). Jesus spent the night on the Mount of Olives. This seems to have been his usual custom when in Jerusalem. Apparently it was not safe for him to remain within the locked gates of the city once the people had dispersed. The next day he returned to the Temple and taught in the room where the offering boxes were placed. Many who heard him believed in him, but others took up stones to throw at him so that Jesus was forced to hide before leaving the Temple. His teachings continued to cause disagreement among the people: 'Many said, "He is possessed, he is raving; why bother to listen to him?" Others said, "These are not the words of a man possessed by a devil: could a devil open the eyes of the blind?"' (Jn 10:19–21 JB).

The following winter Jesus was again in Jerusalem for the Feast of the Dedication. He was walking up and down in the portico of Solomon. 'The Jews gathered around and said, "How much longer are you going to keep us in suspense? If you are the Christ, tell us plainly." Jesus replied: "I have told you, but you do not believe"' (Jn 10:24–25 JB). Again the people took up stones to throw at him but he eluded them and went to the far side of the Jordan where John had baptised. There many of the people came to hear him preach and believed in him.

After Jesus had called Lazarus forth from the tomb some of those present went to the council, warning that if everyone began to follow Jesus, the Romans would destroy the Temple and their nation. It was then that Caiaphas, the high priest, decided it was better that one man should die rather than have the whole nation destroyed. In the eyes of the religious leadership Jesus was not seen as a devout orthodox Jew, but as a religious blasphemer. He no longer went about openly but withdrew to the town called Ephraim situated in an isolated region and there stayed with his disciples. As

the Feast of the Passover approached, the leaders gave orders that
he be found and arrested. However, as Jesus entered the city the
crowds that welcomed him, lining the streets and waving palm
branches, prevented the authorities from taking immediate action.
After preaching to the crowd Jesus again sought refuge knowing
that though he had performed many miracles for them, many did
not believe in him. Yet, we are told that some of the leaders did
believe in him but were afraid to admit it for fear of being expelled
from the synagogues (see Jn 12:12–43). At the Last Supper Jesus
warned the disciples that one of them was about to betray him.
They looked at each other in amazement, then Judas got up and
went out into the night. The Passion of Jesus, with which we are so
familiar, had begun.

Relentlessly throughout the Johannine account, from chapters 5
to 18, Jesus is presented as 'a wanted man'. His life was constantly
under threat and frequently he went into hiding, moving from safe
place to safe place. In the Mark, Luke and Matthew accounts the
first intimation that Jesus' life was in danger came when he
questioned the Sabbath laws. Matthew tells us that after Herod had
John imprisoned, Jesus took the precaution of going to live in
Capernaum, a town outside Herod's jurisdiction. Mark adds the
detail that after the Transfiguration and the cure of the epileptic
boy, Jesus moved about Galilee, not wanting anyone to know where
he was, and warned the disciples that he would be killed. The
Lucan community preserved another detail: when Jesus was
nearing Jerusalem for the last time some Pharisees came out to
meet him. They told him Herod's men were on the lookout to kill
him and advised Jesus to make his getaway while he could.

Apart from living the last years of his life under a death threat
from the religious authorities, the Gospels record that Jesus also
met with rejection from many of the people. Mark describes the
occasion when Jesus returned to Nazareth and preached to the
local people in the synagogue on the Sabbath. They asked, 'Isn't
this the carpenter? Isn't this Mary's son and the brother of James,
Joseph, Judas and Simon? Aren't his sisters here with us? And thy
took offence at him' (Mk 6:3 NIV). Jesus was amazed at their lack
of faith and could work no miracles there. In the Lucan account
this incident is presented more solemnly. Jesus read the mission
statement from Isaiah 61:1–2 and claimed that he had come to
fulfil it. At first the townspeople were amazed at his eloquence and
asked, 'Isn't this Joseph's son?' However, sensing their disbelief
Jesus compared them with Gentile believers in the time of Elijah.

The people were furious at this and rose up, driving Jesus to the edge of the town, intending to throw him over the cliff, but he walked away from them. One wonders how Mary and the family fared in the weeks that followed. Jesus, we know, moved away and settled in Capernaum.

The Nazarenes were not the only people who wanted Jesus out of their town. Once, when he and his disciples took a boat to the east shore of the Sea of Galilee they met an outcast said to be possessed by demons. Jesus exorcised the man and some nearby swine rushed headlong into the lake and were drowned. The herdsmen fled into the town, reporting what had happened. Overcome with fear, the townspeople came out to the lakeside, and they asked Jesus to leave. The people saw the man who was cured, calm and serene, but they did not invite Jesus to stay and heal their sick. Were they more concerned about what may have been an illegal business? Forbidden by the Mosaic law to eat pork, were they secretly herding swine in this isolated place and by night crossing the lake to supply the Roman town of Tiberias with pork? Whatever their reason for rejecting him, Jesus bowed to their wishes and, climbing into the boat, he left the area.

Later when sending his disciples out on mission Jesus would instruct them to shake from their feet the dust of any home or town that would not receive them. There were two towns that apparently welcomed Jesus and had faith in him, for we are told he worked many miracles there; yet we are also told that strangely enough they did not turn from their sins (see Mt. 11:20). These were the towns of Chorazin and Bethsaida, the latter being the home town of Peter and Andrew.

The disciples of John the Baptist came to Jesus and asked why his disciples did not fast when they and the disciples of the Pharisees fasted often. Jesus explained that new wine had to be put into new wineskins. Later he declared that 'John came neither eating nor drinking, and they say, "He has a demon"; the Son of man came eating and drinking, and they say, "Behold, a glutton and a drunkard, a friend of tax collectors and sinners!" Yet wisdom is justified by her deeds' (Mt. 11:18–19 RSV). So here we have even the disciples of John the Baptist harbouring doubts about Jesus.

THE HUMANITY OF JESUS
As tradespeople the family of Jesus would have enjoyed a certain financial independence and in offering a public service would have been known to all and sundry, yet it is hard to surmise what status

they actually held among the people of Nazareth. As we have seen, when Jesus took on a new role and preached for the first time in the local synagogue familiarity with the family contributed in some part to the people's rejection of him. Or put another way, the regard in which the family was held did nothing to gain acceptance for Jesus.

The Johannine account described Jesus as starting his public life at a wedding feast in the neighbouring village of Cana. Further south in Bethany we met him visiting with Martha and Mary and later dining in the house of Simon. As we read the Gospels there emerges the image of Jesus as a sociable person who enjoyed visiting and sharing a meal with his friends.

The Lucan community recalled the incident in Jericho where Jesus invited himself into the home of the tax-collector, Zacchaeus. The Jews despised the tax-collectors because they were Jews in the employ of the Roman conquerors. Together with prostitutes they were regarded as 'public sinners'. When Jesus invited into his company another tax-collector, Matthew, the latter hosted a celebratory feast attended by many tax-collectors and other outcasts. For a Jew to eat from a common dish was a sign that those eating together shared common beliefs and values. The sight of Jesus eating at Matthew's table was a source of scandal for many. When they complained, Jesus said, 'It is not those who are well who need a doctor, but the sick. I have not come to call the virtuous, but sinners to repentance' (Lk. 5:31–32 JB). The Matthean account adds, 'Go and learn the meaning of the words: "What I want is mercy, not sacrifice"' (Mt. 9:13 JB). And so we see that when Jesus set out upon his public ministry he made no calculated effort to gain respectability for himself or for his cause. We also see that, unlike John the Baptist, Jesus was not an ascetic.

One of the first measures Jesus took on going public was to provide himself with a support group, with partners in mission. There were the twelve and the women who accompanied him. Later there were the seventy-two disciples he sent out preaching and healing. His relationship with these companions was just as robust, as were his encounters with his opponents. When in private the disciples asked Jesus to explain his teachings he responded by exclaiming, 'You are no more intelligent than the others' (Mk 7:18 GNB). On coming down from Mount Tabor and being told that the disciples were unable to heal the epileptic boy he said, 'How unbelieving you people are! How long must I stay with you? How long do I have to put up with you? Bring the boy to me!' (Mk 9:19

GNB). His most cutting rebuke was reserved for Peter who tried to dissuade him from facing Jerusalem. Jesus turned on Peter and said, 'Get behind me Satan! Because the way you think is not God's way but man's' (Mk 8:33 JB).

In the Gospels we are shown Jesus displaying opposing emotions. For example in that incident when the Pharisees warned him not to enter Jerusalem, he responded in macho style, 'Go and tell that fox . . . I shall finish my work' (Lk. 13:32 GNB). Then looking down on the city he cried, 'How many times have I wanted to put my arms around all your people, just as a hen gathers her chicks under her wings, but you would not let me!' (Lk. 13:34 GNB). Jesus was not afraid of his emotions and let them surface in response to the various situations in which he found himself. We are told he was filled with pity for a leper, and for the people who followed him to the far side of the Sea of Galilee. He looked on the rich young man with love. At the sight of Mary weeping for her brother Lazarus, Jesus wept. Was he hurt when he was accused of being possessed? The memory seems to have rankled, for at the end of his life he warned the disciples that if he was called Beelzebul, they could expect worse (see Mt. 10:25).

Mark does not hesitate to describe Jesus looking around on the people in anger and being grieved by their lack of compassion (see Mk 3:5). His anger reached peak levels when he observed the trading abuse carried on in the Temple. John records: 'So he made a whip out of cords, and drove all from the temple area . . .' (Jn 2:15 NIV). In contrast John describes Jesus tired and thirsty sitting by the well in Sychar. Mark gives us the picture of a very human Jesus asleep in a boat while a storm rages, and later he describes him rising from table to sing a hymn with his companions before going out to Gethsemane where 'Distress and anguish came over him' (Mk 14:33 GNB).

HANDLING ANGER
Neither Mark nor John hesitated to describe Jesus reacting in anger, for there are situations in which if we failed to be angry we would be morally wanting. Jesus expressed his anger when faced with hypocrisy or a lack of compassion, also when he saw religion reduced to rules and regulations. However, Jesus knew how to handle his anger even as he plaited a whip or overturned the money tables.

The feeling of anger, like pain, is an indicator that something is wrong. Before relief can come, the feeling of anger has to be recognised and acknowledged. This is not an easy matter for some people. A child brought up in an atmosphere in which overt expressions of anger were immediately quashed will have learned by adulthood to suppress the feeling as it arises. In some societies it is acceptable for boys to express anger but not fear, while girls may express fear but not anger.

Suppressed anger cannot be contained. It destroys the person from within and eventually seeps out in the form of nagging, irritability, resentment or anxiety. Its presence can be sensed through some change in the person, she or he starts overeating or drinking, gets unexplained aches and pains, becomes depressed and avoids people. At the root of such anger may be unfulfilled expectations of which the person is not fully aware. It could be a feeling of being undervalued, not being listened to, or of being controlled by another. To be freed from an anger that embitters, it is necessary to trace its hidden source. Then one can decide to use the anger constructively or to laugh at oneself and let it go.

As our feelings arise we initially have no control over them, but once anger is identified decisions need to be made. Anger that is allowed to simmer not only affects the person's health, it also leads to confused, even irrational thinking. Therefore, it is important to regard anger positively, to welcome it as a sign that change is required, maybe in one's own attitudes and behaviour, or in relationships and situations in which one is involved. Anger is not a phase to be endured, rather it is an energising force enabling one to help put a wrong to right. It may be a call to free others from some unfair demands being made upon them, or it may be a social justice issue that urges one to form a pressure group.

Transferred anger is always cowardly. We have all heard of the man who was rebuked by his boss, then went home and shouted at his wife, she in turn nagged the child who went out and kicked the cat. Not only do we at times transfer our anger on to the innocent but we also sometimes fail to identify the real cause of the anger. For example, a parent may express anger with a teenage son who has dyed his hair purple. This becomes the acknowledged issue, but the real source of the anger is anxiety over what the neighbours will think. Again it is unfair to blame another for one's own mood. The statement, 'You make me angry' is not actually correct. 'I let myself become angry with you' is the reality. Just as with violence, anger is never the only response possible.

Recall how anger was expressed in your childhood home. (Was it through violent outbursts, sulks and silences, nagging and belittling others, etc.?)

How was reconciliation achieved?

How is anger expressed in your home today?

When you are angry how does your body respond? (Is it with headaches, stomach cramps, increased heartbeat, etc?)

EXERCISE 1

List two people and two situations that tend to trigger off your anger.

To achieve greater peace of mind and body, against each person and situation write down: a change of attitude you need to make; some positive action you need to take.

EXERCISE 2

Occasionally we are on the receiving end of another's anger.

List what in your behaviour has provoked anger in others.

Complete the sentence: 'When someone is angry with me I . . .'

GOSPEL REFLECTION
If you had been a devout Jew at the time of Jesus and had heard him preach, would you have felt threatened or inspired by him?

Explain your answer.

How would your answer compare with your religious attitudes today?

Sit back and try to imagine:

Jesus as a young man at work in his carpenter's shed;

see him at home with his family;

watch him participating in public worship in the synagogue;

join him enjoying some leisure with his peers;

travel with him and his companions on a journey to Jerusalem.

CLOSING THOUGHT

What message have these twenty-five years of Jesus' private life got for you as you live out your day-to-day life? Think about this quietly for a while.

8

LOVE OTHERS AS YOU LOVE YOURSELF

THE SIN OF LOW SELF-ESTEEM

JESUS MEETS THE DOUBLE STANDARD (JN 8:1–11)
Towards the end of the Feast of Tabernacles Jesus spent the night
out on the Mount of Olives but returned to the Temple early in the
morning. There a number of people gathered around him so he
sat down and began to teach them. Some religious teachers
entered escorting a woman whom they said they had caught in
adultery. She stood before the assembled group. The teachers
pointed out that according to the law of Moses she should be
stoned, then turning to Jesus they asked for his judgment. As they
continued to question him Jesus bent down and with his finger
wrote on the ground. Straightening up he suggested that whoever
among them was without sin should throw the first stone and
bending down again he continued writing. One by one, beginning
with the elders, the men withdrew. Then Jesus looked at the woman
and asked where were her accusers, had any of them condemned
her? None, she told him. Jesus told her to go and sin no more, for
neither would he condemn her.

This story first appeared in issues of Luke's Gospel that were
circulated towards the end of the first century. It was placed in
chapter 20 with the other trap questions put to Jesus, the questions
about paying tax to Caesar and about marriage after the
resurrection. Later it was removed from the Gospel of Luke.
According to Augustine this was in order to avoid scandal. By the
third century the story had been written into chapter 8 of John's
Gospel, where it remains to this day completely out of context with
the surrounding passages, but obviously considered an incident
worth recording for future generations.

In this episode the woman was used to provide a trap question

for Jesus. The religious teachers tried to objectify her, denying her
any personal dignity, but Jesus evaded their planned line of attack
by refusing to discuss the woman's predicament. Instead he turned
the focus away from the woman and onto her accusers by
reminding them of their own sins. In so doing he gave both the
adulteress and the religious teachers a common equality as sinners.
We do not know what Jesus wrote on the ground. We do know,
however, that when Matthew collected the teachings of Jesus he
recorded Jesus as directing his comments about adultery at men,
saying that anyone who lusted after a woman had already
committed adultery with her in his heart. Where women are
perceived purely as sexual objects they are vulnerable to lustful
attacks. Lust is a desire to use another for one's self-gratification
and is a deliberate act. Jesus did not look upon women as a source
of temptation. He is recorded as having women and men disciples
together in his company, for he regarded the sexual impulse as
being within normal human control.

In Simon's house Jesus defended the prostitute who with tears
had washed his feet. He also defended the woman accused of
adultery. There is a difference between the two situations. The first
woman had come to Jesus of her own free will in repentance and
gratitude, and had the courage to disturb an all-male gathering.
This second woman had been dragged into the presence of Jesus
where she confessed no sorrow or repentance yet Jesus did not
condemn her. Was this the scandal Augustine referred to? Jesus
never experienced the sexual vulnerability of a woman, but with
this woman he could share how it felt to be threatened with
stoning.

Matthew also recorded Jesus' warning to those who presumed to
set themselves up as judges of another's morality.

> Do not judge, so that you may not be judged. For with the
> judgment you make you will be judged, and the measure you
> give will be the measure you get. Why do you see the speck in
> your neighbour's eye, but do not notice the log in your own
> eye? Or how can you say to your neighbour, 'Let me take the
> speck out of your eye', while the log is in your own eye? You
> hypocrite, first take the log out of your own eye, and then you
> will see clearly to take the speck out of your neighbour's eye.
> (Mt. 7:1–5 NRSV)

A new Catholic encyclopaedia concludes its section on sin as follows: 'Finally, since external acts are not sure signs of internal dispositions, there is every reason for a non-judgmental attitude towards the neighbour.'[1]

The concern of Jesus was focused on the person of the sinner as someone in need of deliverance from evil desires. He preached repentance. Through repentance the sinner is empowered by the Spirit to live according to the law of God. This law comes written in the heart of all, just as a modern invention comes complete with the maker's instructions. The Council fathers at Vatican II expressed it by saying:

> Deep within their consciences men and women discover a law which they have not laid upon themselves and which they must obey. Its voice, ever calling them to love and to do what is good and to avoid evil, tells them inwardly at the right moment: do this, shun that. For they have in their hearts a law inscribed by God. Their dignity rests in observing this law, and by it they will be judged.[2]

For many women the interpretation of this law written in their hearts proves a problem. The flawed patriarchal culture into which they are born uses power to dominate others. Sin was presented as pride and rebellion against the powers that be. Jesus presented sin as a failure to love, a failure to respect God, and a failure to respect one's neighbour as oneself. Christian women were socialised into practising self-denial long before they had developed any self-esteem, and women passively accepted as virtue what was in fact their failure to be true to their inner selves. This has led them to act like all colonised people who in order to retain some control over themselves become cunning and manipulative, and seldom state openly what they feel and want. People secure in their own self-esteem take responsibility for honest, open relationships and are able to interact with others as equals.

Today many women have come to recognise the presence of sin in their failure to co-operate with the all-empowering Spirit, by remaining passive and unquestioning, and by entertaining a low esteem of self; in other words, by failing to co-operate in achieving their full human potential. As early as the second century Irenaeus, the great defender of Gospel teaching, declared that the glory of God was the human being fully alive. However, in that same century Tertullian labelled women 'sin's gateway' and it was this latter un-Christlike attitude towards women that prevailed among

the Fathers of the early church. When Jesus declined to condemn
the woman accused of adultery and told her to sin no more, was he
enabling her to sense her own dignity and giving her the strength
to be less subservient to the desires of others? Was the root of her
sin to be found in a condition of unquestioning passivity resulting
from low self-esteem?

When writing about this Gospel encounter, John Paul II says:

> The episode recorded in the Gospel of John is repeated in
> countless similar situations in every period of history. A
> woman is left alone, exposed to public opinion with 'her sin',
> while behind 'her' sin there lurks a man – a sinner, guilty 'of
> the other's sin', indeed equally responsible for it. And yet his
> sin escapes notice, it is passed over in silence: he does not
> appear to be responsible for 'the other's sin'! Sometimes,
> forgetting his own sin, he even makes himself the accuser, as
> in the case described.[3]

STUNTED DEVELOPMENT

Children surrounded by people who affirm and accept them grow
up with a great sense of their own self-worth. Having learned to like
themselves they presume that others will like them too, and so they
are open and friendly towards everyone. On the other hand,
children who are constantly criticised and put-down become ill at
ease, are unsure of themselves and keep looking for approval.
Sadly, they learn to be distrustful of others.

Women conditioned to be subservient and passive are full of
self-doubt and have a tendency to undervalue themselves. This
diminishment of self is seen by many women today as being in a
state of sin and in need of redemption. To break the human spirit,
to keep oneself or others in a state of ignorance is to defy God's call
to us to fulfil our human potential.

Women who become chronically passive allow injustices to
flourish. They feel so insecure that they fail to take responsibility
even for their own opinions and preface their views with such
phrases as, 'Jack says . . .' or 'Jill thinks . . .' In constantly seeking
reassurance these women become a burden to those around them.
Yet strange as it may seem, where they have some social advantage
they are capable of considering others as inferior! However, among
their own they feel inadequate and this leaves them open to the
poisonous effects of envy. When a companion is praised the
insecure person feels that she is thereby being judged wanting. The

fear of what others might think so dominates their lives that they give others the right to be their judge. When women become unduly worried about what others think of them, they give others power over them. Their anxiety to be thought well of is for many women the cause of their general discontent with themselves.

HANDLING CRITICISM

Criticism can tell us far more about the critic than about the person criticised. Some criticisms are simply the outpourings of prejudice and jealousy. Some are deliberately vindictive, aimed at enhancing the self at the expense of the other. This results in many people going on the defensive when criticised.

However, criticism can be a sign of respect, of a desire for the betterment of the other. To begin the process of developing self-esteem it is necessary to tackle the fear of criticism. When you are criticised, consider for a moment if what is said is justified, if it is based on fact or is just a personal opinion. For people in the habit of putting themselves down, there is the temptation when criticised to respond in the negative, 'Oh, there I go, stupid again.' Such negative reactions are best avoided. Constructive criticism is always valuable. The self-confident person will receive it with a simple 'Thank you. That is very helpful.' The first time I got this insight into criticism was soon after arriving in Nigeria in 1956. In class I had criticised a twelve-year-old girl. Later when sitting in the study hall waiting for the students to assemble, this girl arrived and came straight up to me. I was surprised as I had expected Irish-style sulks. My surprise increased when she thanked me for the criticism. She said something to the effect that I had acted like a mother, for if I had not cared about her improvement I would not have taken the trouble to point out her faults. There is a truth there.

If the criticism is unjust, put the critic on the spot by asking for a clarification. If you are still not satisfied then defend yourself with self-assurance, saying firmly, 'That criticism was unjustified.' If a criticism is too generalised, such as 'You're always late', make it specific and add a positive statement, for example, 'Yes, I was this time, but I usually take great care to be punctual.' Blanket criticisms such as, 'You're lazy', 'You're very selfish', 'You're so judgmental', leaves the one criticised without any specific attitude or behaviour to start working on. No change can come from such criticism. Similarly to criticise another's stature or mental ability is to criticise them for who they are. To be helpful a criticism needs to be specific and within the person's capacity to effect change.

The worst critic of all is, of course, our inner parent voice which is the residue of the criticisms we received as children. In some societies the negative criticism of children is a cultural norm. Once, when discussing with a group of Dublin women the effects of criticism on children, they each confessed to having criticised their children negatively when talking with neighbours. They had felt it was the socially acceptable thing to do. Then one woman who had taken on the long-term fostering of several children made an interesting confession. She said that when her own children had been admired by others she had always responded with a negative remark, but when a fostered child was admired she had joined in the praise! If we tend to put ourselves and our own down, we will begin to accept as true other people's negative criticisms of us, and worse still we may ourselves become chronically critical of others.

'SIN NO MORE'
Repentance involves undertaking the steps necessary to bring about change. Women who came to like themselves later in life have described the experience as Spirit-filled. In learning to love themselves they were freed of envy, became less judgmental, and developed a greater compassion for others. They felt themselves acquiring Christlike attitudes.

The culture in which we were reared is responsible for many of our present attitudes, but the time comes when as adults we have to take personal responsibility for our attitudes towards God, self and others. Though vindictive criticism is best ignored it is, however, wise to note that praise too can mislead, for some people use praise to gain assent to unwelcome requests. When praise is felt to be deserved and sincerely given, the person with a sense of self-worth will not deflect it but will accept it graciously saying, 'I'm glad you were pleased' or some such words.

Jesus clearly taught that the source of sin lies in our attitudes.

> For it is from within, from the human heart, that evil intentions come: fornication, theft, murder, adultery, avarice, wickedness, deceit, licentiousness, envy, slander, pride, folly. All these evil things come from within, and they defile a person. (Mk 7:21–23 NRSV)

Jesus made it clear that our love of God is expressed through our love of ourselves and of others. By learning to love the divine Spirit and others as ourselves we will reach our full human potential. This calls for women to minister to themselves by deliberately thinking well of themselves. People who learn to accept themselves and others, who appreciate their own and others' gifts and limitations, succeed in acquiring realistic expectations of themselves and others. By taking time to nurture oneself one becomes much better at supporting and affirming others. In the book *Struggle to be Sun Again,* there is a description of how women are transformed from being women of low self-esteem into women capable of social leadership:

> According to Sigrid, women begin to be transformed when they start to appreciate their personhood. Then women need to train themselves in order to equip themselves as effective agents of liberation. Finally, women need to join a larger community of women to sustain their power and make social change possible.[4]

PAUSE FOR REFLECTION

Jesus called people to repentance and to conversion of heart.

Tune in your conscience to the promptings of the Spirit and decide on one attitude you will strive to change.

The fruit of such striving is a greater sense of moral self-worth and inner peace.

EXERCISE 1

List three people with whom you allow yourself to feel inadequate and whose opinions you fear.

In turn, imagine each one in the dock. List possible accusations that could be made against them.

Now decide how in future you will respond when in the company of the people named.

EXERCISE 2

List two positive helpful criticisms you have received.

List two unhelpful criticisms that inhibited you.

For each incident note your response.

In each case how would you respond today?

Resolve to welcome well-meant criticism and to seek feedback from people you trust.

EXERCISE 3

Think back to see if you ever criticised another out of a feeling of jealousy or insecurity.

Recall when you last made a helpful criticism.

Note down what the making of these criticisms tells you about yourself.

GOSPEL REFLECTION
Sit back and relax.

When you are ready read the Gospel passage in which Jesus encounters a woman's accusers (Jn 8:1–11).

Ask the divine Spirit to be with you as you enter into the Temple scene and watch the woman as she is escorted up to Jesus and made to stand before the group he is teaching.

In turn, sense the attitudes of the teachers of religion, of the woman herself, of Jesus, and of some of the individuals among the observers.

What would your attitude have been had you been there?

Try to identify within yourself an attitude of mind that needs to change before it becomes a seed-bed for sinfulness.

Acknowledge your own vulnerability and remain in that mode, aware of the presence of the all-empowering Spirit.

CLOSING THOUGHT
'There must be a renewal in the inner life of your minds; you must be clothed in the new self, which is created in God's image, justified and sanctified through the truth' (Eph. 4:23–24 Knox).

MODEL WOMEN

FACING UP TO CONFLICT AND CONFRONTATION

J esus taught in parables. According to the *Concise Oxford Dictionary* a parable is a 'narrative of imagined events used to typify moral or spiritual relations'. So far we have reflected on Jesus relating to some of the women he met during his public life of healing and teaching. Now we are going to meet two women who appear in the parables and who were created entirely from Jesus' imagination. Not only did he create them, but he presented them to us as models of womanly behaviour. In studying these parables we get a further glimpse into the mind of Jesus and his attitude towards women.

THE PARABLE OF THE WIDOW AND THE JUDGE (LK. 18:1–8)
There was a judge who no longer feared either God or the people. In the same city there lived a widow who went to the judge seeking justice against an opponent. The judge refused to act. The widow returned again and again to plead her case. Worn out by her persistence and not wishing to be disturbed further, this unjust judge finally acted and justice was done.

Notice that Jesus presents this woman as acting out of the most vulnerable position possible for a woman in the Israel of his time, that of a lone widow. A woman without a husband, son or male relative to act for her was without influence, could be brushed aside and not listened to. Such treatment eventually causes the victims to become passive, and to avoid drawing attention to themselves as they quietly eke out an existence.

The widow envisaged by Jesus did not become passive, even when faced with a new opponent in the person of a corrupt judge. A judge is one of the most influential members of a community, entrusted with the power to see that justice is maintained. According to the parable the judge knew that the widow had a just cause, but having a just cause did not secure justice for her. It was the woman's own character and behaviour that brought about a just resolution. It was not a sense of justice that caused the judge to act, but the nuisance caused by an assertive woman.

This woman knew the law, knew that right was on her side. Such knowledge breeds confidence, some say such knowledge *is* power. She was asking not for a favour but for justice, and it was justice for herself, a thing many women find it impossible to ask for. They find it much easier to seek justice for another. The way she went about achieving her rights was straightforward and open. She was not manipulative, did not play at being helpless. Instead she was prepared to be persistent, to be perceived as a nuisance and to suffer rejection again and again, until finally her moral strength forced the judge to carry out his duty. Throughout she was not intimidated but retained her integrity. Such behaviour was commended by Jesus. Nor was this assertive widow a one-off in the mind of Jesus. Earlier in Luke's Gospel Jesus from out of his imagination had created another woman who refused to remain passive when faced with a difficulty. She had lost one of her ten silver coins, so she lit a lamp and searched until she found it, then she called her neighbours and rejoiced with them (Lk. 15:8–10).

Jesus presented this woman as imaging God's concern for sinners. Obviously Jesus had no problem in having a woman image God. It is also interesting to note that Jesus had her searching not for a lost child or a lost lamb, but for money, her dowry perhaps and her only financial security.

In real life Jesus had met such a persevering woman. She was a Gentile who pleaded for her daughter to be cured, even when the disciples tried to have her sent away, and even when Jesus himself seemed to reject her (see Chapter 6). She acted on behalf of her daughter, but the women Jesus presented in the parables acted on behalf of themselves.

In giving us this powerful, vulnerable widow, Jesus has given us a model of a woman who knew her rights and knew also that she had a duty to exercise them. In his encyclical *Pacem in Terris* Pope John XXIII wrote:

> Women are gaining an increasing awareness of their natural dignity. Far from being content with a purely passive role, or allowing themselves to be exploited, they are demanding

both in domestic and in public life the rights and duties which belong to them as human persons.

He went on to add: 'The possession of rights involves the duty of implementing those rights . . . '[1] When women associate self-love with selfishness, and self-assertion with sinfulness, they are failing to live up to the models of womanhood given to us by Jesus himself.

A LIFE OF PRAYER

Jesus told this parable in order to exhort his listeners not to be discouraged and to pray always. Obviously, Jesus was not here talking about public worship or the saying of prayers, but of becoming prayerful people who live lives of prayer. When Matthew gathered some key teachings of Jesus into the Sermon on the Mount he recorded Jesus as saying, 'It is not those who say to me, "Lord, Lord", who will enter the kingdom of heaven, but the person who does the will of my Father in heaven' (Mt. 7:21 JB). In the last sermon recorded by Matthew, Jesus declares that it is through just and compassionate behaviour towards the poor, the sick and the imprisoned that we enter into a right relationship with God (see Mt. 25:31–46). This sermon echoes the one with which Jesus started his public life in Nazareth when he proclaimed that his role was to bring good news to the poor, to heal the sick and liberate the oppressed. The *Modern Catholic Encyclopedia,* under the heading 'Praying Always', says:

> In a truly Christian life, there is no moment, no act which is not prayer. One's whole life becomes prayer. Prayer penetrates the entire day every day. In this fashion, prayer is a hope, an expectancy, a conscious awareness of his (God's) real presence. Life in prayer is life doing the work of Christ, is awareness that everything is gift and grace, is recognition of others as a presence of Christ.[2]

In other words, for the Christian a life of prayer is a life of action in which Christ's mission to promote the Reign of God is continued.

The oppressed widow was given to us by Jesus as a model of how to pray. Co-operating with the empowering presence of the Spirit within her, her mode of prayer was to persevere in persisting that justice be done. In the parable the corrupt judge could not possibly represent God; therefore, the widow is not engaged in making prayers of petition. Rather, throughout the parable the presence of God is sensed within the moral strength of the vulnerable one.

CONFLICT IS INEVITABLE AMONG HUMANS

Conflict is neither good nor bad. In fact it can have positive effects by clearing the atmosphere and providing an opportunity to clarify a present situation and to make realistic decisions for the future.

Most conflicts arise from misunderstandings which become issues when one feels threatened as regards one's reputation, quality of life, religious beliefs, ambitions, and even one's dreams. It is important to recognise the signs of conflict and this is easily done, as conflict generates negative responses. Either oneself or the other feels hurt, fearful or resentful and this will show in a change of behaviour when one person becomes angry, stubborn or starts avoiding the other. Once aware that conflict exists it is better to acknowledge the fact and try to deal with it, otherwise it will fester and become more difficult to resolve. This is best done when emotions have calmed down. In relationships the cause of a difficulty never lies just with one side but in the combined attitudes of both and the interaction between them. It takes moral courage to act. It is wise, therefore, to start overcoming any fear one might have of conflict and learn to see it as a positive human experience.

We can learn to deal with conflict. First get rid of any fear of the other. Then examine one's own attitudes and behaviour to see how much they have contributed to the situation. Become aware of one's tendency to be aggressive, to blame or to play the victim. Make sure that any demands to be made are reasonable by focusing only on what can be changed, that is on behaviour and attitudes, not on the character or personality of the person. Remember the past cannot be changed and be patient, as it takes time to acquire new attitudes and to alter behaviour.

Whether the conflict is between two adults or an adult and a child, it is important that the other be treated with respect. This means not presuming to know the other's views and motivation, but to be ready to listen, to allow the other to pour out grievances real or imagined. The aim is to understand the other's fears and perceptions. If there is no willingness to understand, an acceptable solution cannot be reached. However, such willingness has to be on both sides. Therefore, it may be necessary to insist on being heard and having one's own needs considered. These should be prioritised, so that while respecting the needs of the other there is a limit to how far one is willing to acquiesce.

Preparation is essential; if you are first approached by the other, ask for time before entering into discussion. Write down the facts and be sure to distinguish between facts and presumptions. Then sit back and imagine yourself during the exchange, hear the tone of your voice, see your bearing and facial expression, become aware of your feelings. Such preparation should protect you against being provoked into responding aggressively or going on the defensive.

During the encounter there is no value in losing one's temper, belittling or blaming the other. The work of the discussion is to define the problem, suggest possible solutions, and to agree on one to follow. If one person cannot face up to conflict, the other is left with the burden of trying to conduct the process of conflict resolution as far as is possible. The extent of the other's anger or dismissiveness indicates the depth of the hurt or the lack of interest in the relationship. If justice is to be done it may be necessary to seek outside assistance. This is what the widow in the parable did and found her problem had become twofold, but empowered by the Spirit justice was achieved. There are situations in which failure to seek justice is to fail to act as a disciple of the Christ.

JESUS AND CONFLICT

Jesus experienced conflict throughout his public life. Sometimes he deliberately brought the conflict to a head, as when he healed on the Sabbath and provoked the wrath of his religious leaders, but at the same time succeeded in establishing the priority of compassion over religious regulations. At other times it was he who was approached, as when a teacher of the law tried to trap him with a question on how best to gain eternal life. Jesus responded with a parable, and in turn trapped the lawyer into admitting that a Samaritan could prove more worthy than a priest or Levite. However, it may be a consolation to some to realise that at times Jesus chose not to seek a resolution to the conflict. There was the occasion in his home town when the Nazarenes sought to stone him and he decided on avoidance rather than confrontation. Twice there were similar incidents in the Temple, when again Jesus withdrew. On one of these occasions he removed himself to beyond the Jordan.

In his teachings Jesus challenged the traditional stance on justice, an eye for an eye and a tooth for a tooth. He denounced any notion of revenge. If in a no-win situation, he recommended keeping oneself in control of the situation by offering one's coat when one's shirt is taken; or if a soldier in the army of occupation forces one to carry his pack one mile, willingly to carry it a second. It is one way of coming through one's ordeal both mentally and emotionally intact.

VARIOUS STANCES POSSIBLE IN CONFLICT

The stance taken in conflict depends on how serious one considers the situation or values the relationship involved. If one feels physically threatened and has good reason to believe the other's views are entrenched, then avoidance may be the sensible option. If one is anxious to retain the relationship at all cost, perhaps because of one's emotional or financial dependence on the other, then the usual response is acceptance of the situation. Unfortunately; in both of these circumstances resentment can build up and eat away at the person. For the preservation of one's sanity it is important to realise that one has made the choice to avoid or to accept and then to let the issue go, to live without guilt or hatred. When the situation or the relationship is not considered important the difficulty is often left to drift. Again a choice has been made, this time to do nothing. Therefore, it is wise to smile at the difficulty and not allow it to develop into a major irritant.

Where there is a commitment to the common good, then divisive issues need to be resolved. Compromise is probably the short-term solution. Each side has to hold firm to its priority needs while calming the fears of the other by yielding on some issues. The weakness of a compromise lies in the fact that some issues are left unresolved. Its strength lies in the time it allows for understanding and trust to grow so that the remaining issues may be dealt with at a later date. Of course, the ideal is achieved when both sides regard conflict as morally neutral and as affording a normal growth point in a relationship or situation. Both acknowledge there is a difficulty and are anxious to understand each other's fears. They enter the discussion determined to solve the problem together.

THE QUEEN OF SHEBA MEETS KING SOLOMON (1 KGS 10:1–13)

Chapter 9 of the first book of Kings ends with a description of Solomon's fleet sailing the coast of North Africa and returning with its holds filled with gold. When the Queen of Sheba heard of the fame of Solomon she travelled to Jerusalem to put some 'hard questions' to the king. She arrived with a large retinue and with camels carrying spices, gold and precious stones. On meeting the king she discussed all her concerns with him and Solomon was able to answer all her questions. The queen was greatly impressed by

Solomon's wisdom, his palace, his care for and organisation of his staff, and his offerings in the Temple. She admitted that she had not believed all that she had heard of him, but now that she had come and seen with her own eyes his wisdom and the happiness of his people, she thanked God for entrusting him with the exercise of justice. They exchanged gifts and the king granted the queen all that she desired.

So important was this event to the Jews that it was recorded again in 2 Chr. 9:1–12. Sixteen hundred years later the incident was once more recorded, this time in *The Koran* by the prophet Muhammed. According to this account Solomon was told that the people of Saba (Sheba) had '. . . a woman reigning over them, gifted with everything, and she hath a splendid throne. . . .' On hearing this, Solomon sent a letter to the queen threatening to invade the country unless she surrendered her realm. The queen called her nobles and asked their advice, but they replied: 'We are endued with strength and are endued with mighty valour – But to command is thine.' The queen answered, 'Kings when they enter a city spoil it, and abase the mightiest of its people; and in like manner will these also do.'[3]

Some modern commentators support this version by stating,

> More prosaically, the queen's visit was a punitive expedition, to put a stop to interference with her lucrative India-to-Canaan spice monopoly. His 'wisdom' which she so outspokenly admired in verse 6, doubtless consisted in a canny merger guaranteeing increased profits to them both.[4]

Sheba or Saba is believed to have been in the area of Yemen. If so, the Queen of Sheba set up firm trading contracts, for from the twelfth to the first centuries BC the land and its people enjoyed great prosperity. Their wealth depended on the camel caravans that traded all over the peninsula and northwards into the Middle East. When the Phoenician sailors finally discovered sea routes to the Indian Ocean, the desert trade declined. However that may be, the Ethiopian royal family claims descent from an offspring born of a union between Solomon and the Queen of Sheba. They therefore maintain that Sheba was sited in Ethiopia. The Jewish historian Josephus, writing in the first century AD, presumed that the Queen of Sheba was black, thus giving support to the Ethiopian claim.

The Scripture writers present the Queen of Sheba as a woman

capable of exercising public responsibility. If indeed her visit to King Solomon was one of confrontation, she undertook it with tact and courage, meeting him as an equal. She was not content with rumours but took the trouble to travel out of her own country in order to meet and understand her potential enemy. She did not act alone but brought others with her. She had done her research well, so that along with trading gifts she had ready some relevant questions, and it is recorded that she asked them in an open and forthright manner. Despite the Ethiopean claims, the Scriptures give no indication that this Gentile woman acted in a manipulative or seductive way. For her, wisdom was found not only in wise sayings but in a person's whole lifestyle and capacity for good relationships. This she recognised as the work of God and gave thanks. Then with wisdom equal to the King's, she succeeded in gaining his co-operation to the benefit of both their peoples.

CONFRONTATION

Confrontation has been described as strong love. One needs to care about the relationship or the issue at stake before one makes the effort to confront. It is an acquired skill having the opposite aim to that of debate. In debate one listens in order to undermine the arguments of the other. In confrontation one listens in order to understand the other's needs and fears, with the aim of reaching a mutually satisfying agreement.

The attitude with which one enters into confrontation is all-important and remains in one's control no matter who initiates the confrontation. The encounter takes place between equals, neither party is on trial, there is no judge. One simply recognises that there is a problem and that it is not just mine or yours, but ours. So one enters into confrontation in order to understand the other's views and to have one's own views heard. This requires speaking the truth openly. Some people regard speaking the whole truth as insensitive, as lacking in kindness, but it is more likely to be a lack of trust in the other's honesty. To confront others is not to affront them. There is no room for an 'I win – you lose' attitude, or even for an unhappy compromise; rather it is a question of both sides being willing to stay in communication until a mutual acceptance has been reached. The attitude is that of acknowledging a mutual problem which will be solved together, of working towards an 'I win – you win' outcome.

To achieve a satisfactory conclusion it is important to keep in mind the necessity of acting for the good of both sides. Approach the problem as a mutual difficulty. The fears of both need to be stated and steps taken to minimise them. Isolate the symptoms so that you can concentrate on actually identifying and defining the problem. Each party is responsible for prioritising its own needs and for seeing together where they might support each other. List possible solutions and cross out the least agreeable. Decide on which to implement. Set a time-limit for re-evaluation and be prepared to make adjustments. Remaining differences often open up new perspectives and prove to be mutually enriching.

The Queen of Sheba set out with questions to ask the King. Sometimes questions can be trap-questions, as Jesus often experienced.

'Don't you think that . . .', restricts the person's response. 'But didn't you say . . .', does not contribute to seeking the truth. For meaning is not found in the words alone, but also in the emotions and tone of voice, as well as in the context in which the statement was made. 'When will you . . .', is often a covert demand. 'Why can't you . . .'; 'Why' questions can be manipulative and are often best responded to, Jesus-like, with another question.

Strong caring love is not out to set traps. It is always wisest to make 'I' statements: 'I fear . . .', 'I need . . .', 'I thought . . .', 'I understood . . .', 'I felt . . .', and never to embark on 'You' statements: 'You fear . . .', 'You want . . .', 'You think . . .', 'You meant . . .', etc. When deciding to confront, another one of the risks involved is that of discovering that you were in the wrong all the time!

PEACE-MAKING

Confrontation is central to all peace-making. Peace-makers do not go off into desert places to commune alone with God. They are to be found wherever conflict and misunderstandings are destroying right relationships and they are prepared to stay there with the hurt and the pain. Peace-makers take risks, face challenges, overcome prejudice, and are sometimes looked upon as trouble-makers themselves, for they tend to bring injustices out into the open. For Christians, peace-making is at the core of continuing Christ's mission on earth.

INTERDEPENDENCE

The work of confrontation and reconciliation is very demanding and is best undertaken with the help of like-minded people. Jesus himself gave us the example of working with a group. It is said that as children we are totally dependent, as adolescents we strive for independence, but as adults we realise wholeness is achieved through interdependence. We come to recognise and accept our limitations and to appreciate the richness of talents, skills, knowledge and experience available to us when we work as a team, not to mention the emotional support we receive through human companionship. The Christian understanding of the Godhead as trinitarian and in whose image we are created, indicates that ours is to be a more social spirituality that is globally aware and capable of entering into the mind and vision of Christ.

Let us for a moment try to enter into the mind of the boy Jesus. As a child growing up in Nazareth, he would have gone daily to the synagogue to learn Hebrew and the history of God's dealings with his people. He would have learned the psalms and prophets by rote and heard the great stories of Moses, Samuel, David and Solomon. One day he would have reached the story of the Queen of Sheba's visit to the royal palace. He would have learned of Solomon's fleet and the Queen's camel caravans plying their trade across sea and desert. He would have learned the names of the spices from the Orient, the wonderful woods brought to build the Temple, the gold and the precious stones. And he might have wondered what were those hard questions that she asked of the king. (Later he himself, while still a boy, would ask searching questions of the rabbis in that same Jerusalem.)

Did he return home with his head full of the Queen of Sheba story and insist on telling it all over again to his mother and anyone else who would listen to him? We do not know. But what we do know is that the story of the courageous journey undertaken by the queen in order to seek wisdom, understanding of and co-operation with a neighbour for the good of their people inspired Jesus during his few short years of adult life. He must have thought of her often during his years of public teaching, for she came spontaneously to his mind when some Pharisees and teachers of the law challenged him to perform a miracle. He refused, pointing out that it was not through miracles that one was saved but through repentance, as shown by the pagan people of Nineveh in response to the word of the prophet Jonah, and through seeking wisdom. Then he declared: 'The Queen of the South will rise at the judgment with this generation and condemn it; for she came from the ends of the earth to listen to Solomon's wisdom, and now one greater than Solomon is here' (Mt. 12:42 NIV).

Jesus has given us this Gentile woman as a model by which to measure our own performance in life. Obviously, she had made an impression on him. What was it that he admired in her? Was it her own sense of dignity and equality as she carefully chose her gifts and set out with her advisers to meet the king? Was it the mental ability with which she assessed information and prepared shrewd questions? Was it her willingness and courage to risk undertaking a hazardous journey into another territory in order to confront a potential enemy and strive to attain mutual understanding? Was it because she was open to learn from another, to listen to new insights and gain a wider perspective? Whatever it was, Jesus has given to us, men and women, the Queen of Sheba as a model for human behaviour. She accepted personal responsibility and used the potential of the situation into which she was born. In so doing she promoted God's reign on earth.

PAUSE FOR REFLECTION
What for you is the lesson of the parable of the widow and the judge?

What difference is there between the concept of God as all-powerful, and God as all-empowering?

EXERCISE 1

Recall the style of conflict resolution practised in your home when you were young. In one sentence state how it has influenced your present attitude towards conflict.

EXERCISE 2

On a separate sheet of paper complete these sentences:

When in conflict with an elder I . . .

When in conflict with my spouse I . . .

When in conflict with a child I . . .

When in conflict with a friend I . . .

When in conflict with a person in authority I . . .

When in conflict with a stranger I . . .

What have you learned about yourself from the above exercise?

EXERCISE 3

Spend tomorrow without attributing motives to or making presumptions about people you know and public figures. Think and state only facts.

EXERCISE 4

Relax and allow to surface in your mind a personal situation you find negative, even distressing, and would like to resolve. It may be a serious relationship problem or a minor irritation at work or in the home. Prepare to confront the situation. Decide on the attitudes you need to develop and try to discover your own motivation. Plan the venue in which to act, the statements you will make and the questions you want to ask.

Then sit back and in imagination watch yourself as you carry out the process.

How do you feel right now?

If you feel empowered to act, ask the Spirit to act with you.

If you feel you cannot face the hassle then let go of the situation and take responsibility for your decision. Perhaps you now see the minor irritation as amusing. Perhaps you have decided to accept the relationship as it is, or to keep it politely at arm's length. Remember that the avoidance solution always leaves a sense of unfinished business. Whatever the decision, ask God to bless the person or persons concerned and let go of any anxiety.

GOSPEL REFLECTION

The Queen of Sheba was an historical character about whom Jesus heard when he was a small boy. Later, in creating his own characters to give us as models, he described a widow who confronted a judge, a woman who took vigorous action to recover her lost wealth, young women who were capable of saying 'No.'

Sit back, relax and recall the many Gospel images of Jesus talking *about* women and *to* women.

List qualities you think Jesus admired in women.

Imagine yourself at the end of your life coming into the presence of Christ and finding him standing with the Queen of Sheba by his side. Look steadily into the eyes of both.

Stay in this situation for a while.

Then describe what happened.

CLOSING PRAYER
Ask the Spirit to be with all international peace-makers.

Within the closer circle of family, friends and acquaintances name those in need of reconciliation. Ask the Spirit to empower each one and to lead them into the way of peace.

10

PRAYING WITH FEW WORDS

ATTENTIVE LISTENING

Perhaps the most peace-promoting activity we can engage in is that of listening to another. It has been said that most conflict is the result of misunderstandings, of making assumptions and not taking time to listen in order to understand the fears, needs and presumptions of the other.

ATTENTIVE LISTENING

Attentive listening is one of the greatest gifts we can offer to another. Good listening says: 'I respect you, find you interesting.' All of us – child, youth, man, woman, elder, stranger – need to feel worthwhile if we are to enjoy life to our full human potential.

I remember once listening to a radio phone-in on which a psychologist was taking questions. A nine-year-old girl explained that her baby brother would be a year old that week and she wanted to know what was the best toy to get him. The psychologist advised her to forget the toy and instead to give her brother half an hour of undivided attention, adding that there was nothing infants needed more than to feel wanted and to see another enjoy their company. This reminded me of a housebound woman who received the services of meals-on-wheels volunteers and of Eucharistic ministers. She said that at times she would willingly forgo the dinner and even Holy Communion if only the person would stay awhile and talk with her.

Today, attentive listening is recognised as a source of healing. It has actually developed into the profession of counselling. Attentive listening is one of the best means of affirming another. When joys are shared they are doubled. When negative feelings are heard they have a chance to heal and make way for more positive attitudes.

Just as a person takes measures to prepare a comfortable room for a visitor, so the attentive listener clears a space in the mind, sets aside personal concerns and stray thoughts and offers the hospitality of the mind and heart by giving full attention to the other. This is an acquired skill. One can learn to switch off one's own preoccupations in order to listen to another. Once a person feels heard, understood and respected, self-confidence and trust develop and the person is freed to grow. The alternative is withdrawal, a sense of rejection, of failure.

Attentive listening is life-enhancing. The experience of being truly listened to enables a person to grow in self-esteem and to clear the mind of self-deprecating attitudes or undermining grudges. The person goes away feeling a new sense of well-being.

THE MINISTRY OF ATTENTIVE LISTENING

Whether standing listening to someone in a casual street encounter, or seated visiting with a friend, whether alone with the person or in a group at a meeting, a family meal or a party, the process is the same. The good listener shows contentment at being with the person by immediately relaxing the body, looking at the speaker, establishing eye contact and concentrating on what is being said. Have you ever noticed that in a group there is sometimes a person who cannot get a word in, is constantly ignored. The person is left with a dull feeling of frustration and a sense of being excluded. Anyone present who appreciates the contribution that listening makes to another's wholeness will see to it that such a person is given space, or will engage them in private conversation later. With practice, attentive listening becomes a most rewarding gift but at first it can prove an exacting form of loving.

Good listeners resist the temptation to interrupt, to take over the conversation by recounting similar experiences. They wait until the speaker has finished before responding. In fact they show interest and encourage the other to go on talking by giving one-word responses such as, 'Gosh', 'Really?', 'Sorry', etc. Or they ask short open-ended questions which help the speaker to continue: 'What happened next?', 'How did you feel about that?' They will never make judgmental statements. 'There was no need for you . . .' only puts the speaker on the defensive. 'That's nothing to worry about' simply makes people feel they are not being taken seriously. To the statement 'If I was you I would have . . .', I heard one woman reply, 'That's not true. If you were me you would have done exactly as I did.' Probing questions can also be off-putting. 'Why did you do that?' makes people feel they are on trial. In trying to explain they may lose their line of thought and never get to say what they really wanted to say.

Yet there are occasions when the 'Why?' question helps the speaker to become aware of negative attitudes. The good listener is content to be a sounding board off which the other can bounce conflicting thoughts. Nor is he or she uncomfortable with pauses, but simply waits until the other is ready to proceed. Even when advice is asked it is seldom wanted of course, and if given it can leave the adviser open to future blame. Information is usually helpful, with perhaps some suggestions; but helping people to reach their own conclusions is always best. Ask, 'What options are open to you?', 'What do you feel you would like to do?', or any question that helps people to think out solutions for themselves. Note: if you cannot understand the person because of accent or low voice, say so, but make it out to be your problem and not theirs.

We communicate simultaneously at several levels. First there are the words used, the tone of voice, the rate of delivery; then there is the non-verbal body language, the leaning forward or half-turning away, the shrug, the frown, the smile, the sneer, the nervous laugh, the look of affection and so on. This means several messages go out at the same time. Usually they reinforce the same message but at times they are contradictory. This latter situation can cause misunderstandings, especially for children and foreigners. If we are not aware of this we can send out a message not intended. Therefore, I always feel it is better to avoid the words, 'But you said . . .' There was more to the communication than what was said. The person might have been teasing, or pressurised into saying what was said, yet sent clear messages of reluctance, etc.

No matter what the topic, emotions, positive or negative, are being expressed all the time. The attentive listener learns to tune in to the feelings of the other. The alert listener matches the other's level of feeling, light-hearted with the light-hearted, serious with the serious. The effect is summed up in the Eastern saying: 'The children of God go about making the sad happy and the happy happier.' Sometimes people talk just to 'let off steam', they are simply communicating feelings, not facts, and do not expect an intellectual response. While listening to another, it is important to become aware of one's own feelings, to see if they are governed by affection for the person or by prejudice, etc.

Attentive listening inspires deep sharing. There is a danger here, as the speaker may communicate more than intended. If this is suspected, interrupt the flow with a question requiring a clarification such as, 'What did you mean when you said . . . ?' or 'When did this happen?' This diverts the speaker and puts a brake on the direction the conversation is taking. The speaker is given time to privately decide whether to continue sharing or to change the subject. If the person continues to share intimately the listener is faced with another problem. On parting, the person may feel embarrassed and be left the worse for the conversation. If you as the listener allow the speaker to continue at this level, then in charity you may need to contribute some sharing yourself so that the other can go away with a sense of mutuality.

You may have a friend who stays on the phone for hours on end or keeps you standing in the street till your feet ache and it is always about the same gripe. This is a serious situation and many of the women I have met who have such a friend fail to act firmly, believing such a course would be unkind. Yet when you listen to a person repeat the 'chip on their shoulder' over and over again you are reinforcing their bitterness. Hear your friend out once, then twice if necessary. After that the most helpful response is to say something like, 'You have told me this twice already. You may have no power to change the situation but it is in your power to change your attitude towards it. So what practical steps can you take?' From then on only discuss the stages in the progress out of the situation. Soon your friend will be emotionally free unless he or she is enjoying their misery, in which case a new listener will be found and you will hear no more about that particular grievance.

Older children and teenagers often 'test the waters' before confiding. 'Anything good on telly tonight?' The mood of the response will decide whether a conversation proceeds. To stop what you are doing and to establish eye contact before answering can hugely influence the quality of communication between the young and the older person. If you feel excluded from the thoughts of the younger people in your life, you may need to question your initial listening responses. 'You never listen' is a common complaint among the young. Are they right?

There are times and circumstances when it is not convenient to give full attention. Again, many older women find this a difficult situation to handle. They may ease themselves away leaving the other feeling hurt and themselves guilty, while in fact, if there is guilt, it belongs with the other for imposing or being thoughtlessly demanding. It is not always possible to be free to listen on demand.

Therefore, explain the situation, make a future appointment if necessary and leave it at that without harbouring any guilt. You may have a previous commitment, or are not feeling well, or are just too tired to listen.

Another danger area is remaining silent after listening. This can lead to misunderstandings if the person presumes that you have agreed with all that was said. I believe a listener has a responsibility to briefly affirm or disagree. To disagree is a sign of treating the other with respect, of letting her or him know they are being taken seriously and not just being humoured. The ministry of listening is as important as that of preaching. Through good listening the Spirit's healing grace can flow.

Our capacity to listen to another is the same as our capacity to listen to God. It is the yardstick by which we can measure the quality of our prayer. People who have not given time to the meditative side of prayer may become compulsive workers in their desire to serve God. Compulsive activity can stunt spiritual growth. Jesus was not a workaholic. Even the Gospels which focus on his public life show him taking time out for leisure and for private prayer. Learn to recognise when you have need of a listener. It is part of our trust in God's care for us to seek the Spirit present and at work in others.

JESUS AT PRAYER

We have already seen that Jesus was conscientious about attending public worship, whether in the local synagogue or in the Temple where sacrifice was offered. Let us now look at Jesus as he engaged in private prayer.

The Gospels of Mark, Matthew and Luke present Jesus preparing for his public ministry by first going out into the desert to pray and fast for forty days. These passages recall the forty years spent by Moses and the Israelites in the desert. Like the Hebrews of old, Jesus was accompanied by the Spirit. There in the desert he was tempted – as is all humanity – and he had to struggle against his human desires for wealth, power and honour. He was well aware of the popular expectation of a Messiah king who as a powerful political leader would restore independence and prosperity to his nation. Later in his public life these temptations would come back to haunt him, as when the Zealots tried to make him king, or when the crowds followed him seeking bread.

The Jews understood sickness and poverty to be the result of sin, a sign of God's displeasure. Health and prosperity were interpreted as a sign of God's favour. This was the mind-set that Job had to deal with. Even among the disciples of Jesus the same views held. On meeting a blind man they asked, 'Teacher, whose sin caused him to be born blind? Was it his own or his parents' sin?' (Jn 9:2 GNB). Jesus rejected such notions. For him the true bread was found not in prosperity but in the word of God which nourishes and enhances life. In his desert struggle Jesus turned his back on the alluring prospect of a royal messiahship and instead followed the role of the teaching prophet which traditionally ended in suffering and death.

Again and again it is reported that Jesus withdrew into a quiet place to pray. 'Then, at very early dawn, he left them, and went away to a lonely place, and began praying there' (Mk 1:35 Knox). 'And he would steal away from them into the desert and pray there' (Lk. 5:16 Knox). 'It was at this time he went out onto the mountainside, and passed the whole night offering prayer to God' (Lk. 6:12 Knox). These withdrawals occurred after a long day of healing, or when he was about to make an important decision such as choosing the twelve. Later Jesus would bring some of the twelve up Mount Tabor or into the garden of Gethsemane to be near him while he prayed.

JESUS' TEACHING ON PRAYER

There was obviously something special about Jesus when he was engaged in private prayer, and when the disciples became aware of this they asked him to teach them to pray in like manner. Now these were Jews trained in ritual prayer since childhood, so it was something more they asked of Jesus. He told them,

> When you pray, you are to say, Father, hallowed be thy name; thy kingdom come; give us this day our daily bread; and forgive us our sins; we too forgive all those who trespass against us; and lead us not into temptation. (Lk. 11:2–4 Knox)

Jesus then went on to recommend perseverance: ask, seek, knock. He compared God to an earthly father who, when asked by his child for bread, would not give a stone, or for a fish would not give a snake, or for an egg would not give a scorpion. In this way Jesus encouraged the disciples to see in God a loving parent always ready to give to those who ask. But according to the Lucan account what God is always ready to give is not bread, fish or eggs but the all-empowering Spirit (see Lk. 11:5–13).

The teaching on prayer as passed down in the Matthean community starts with Jesus warning the disciples against behaving like those hypocrites who stood and prayed in the synagogues and on the street corners where all might see them. The disciples were taught to pray in private behind closed doors unseen by all save God alone. Jesus also instructed them not to do as the heathens, who through long prayers hoped to make themselves heard. The disciples were to use few words, as God knew their needs even before they asked. They were simply to say:

> Our Father, who art in heaven, hallowed be thy name; thy kingdom come; thy will be done, on earth as it is in heaven; give us this day our daily bread; and forgive us our trespasses, as we forgive them that trespass against us; and lead us not into temptation, but deliver us from evil. Amen. (Mt. 6:9–13 Knox)

The Matthean version of Jesus' teaching on prayer has become a formula used by all Christians. As Luke and Matthew handed down two different versions, it was presumably seen by the early Christians not as a formula of words, but as a list of the attitudes with which we should approach God.

First, we are to regard God as a loving parent. Here Jesus is dispelling fear and encouraging intimacy: 'Abba', that is 'Papa' or today's 'Dad'. Most Christians have no problem in approaching God as their life-giving source. The difficulty arises with the implication. If God is my parent then everyone else is my sister and brother. Jesus made this clear when he insisted that all who lived according to the will of God were his sisters and brothers. In approaching God in prayer we have to entertain goodwill towards all. We have to overcome our prejudices and our tendency to judge others.

Then we are to be aware of the transcendence of God and to be willing to co-operate with the Spirit in promoting the reign of God on earth through striving for justice and peace. Next we trust in God to provide for our needs. The early Christians saw this happening in their willingness to share what they possessed and through caring for each other with compassionate love. (In the constitutions of my religious community under the section dealing with the vow of poverty it is written: 'Through our dependence on the community we both express, and are helped to grow in, our dependence upon God.'[1] Of course, each one contributes according to her talents and abilities, so that dependence on God is expressed through interdependence on each other. In the larger community of the nation this interdependence continues, as we urge our governments to pass just tax and wage laws and to provide an adequate social welfare system.) The most demanding of the attitudes expressed in the 'Our Father . . .' is when we ask for forgiveness in the measure that we are willing to forgive others. Finally we are to trust the all-empowering Spirit to bring us through hard times and difficult situations.

So for Jesus private prayer is the means by which we transform our way of life and bring our attitudes into alignment with those of God. Through prayer we are empowered to play our part in contributing to the spread of God's reign of compassionate justice on earth.

FORGIVENESS

The Matthean account of Jesus' teaching on prayer ends by repeating once more the essential attitude of forgiveness. Unless we are prepared to forgive those who have offended us, there is no point in approaching God in prayer or in asking to have forgiven the wrongs that we commit. It is easier to forgive others when we acknowledge that we too have offended. The Matthean community emphasised the importance of this attitude when they recalled Jesus saying that if on the way to the altar you remember someone has something against you, turn back and be reconciled first with that person before returning to the altar.

The great story of forgiveness, told by Jesus, is that of a father and his two sons. The younger son, unwilling to wait for his father's death, asked for his inheritance in advance. The father gave it to him, so he packed up and went to a distant city where he squandered all he had. His new-found friends then deserted him and he, a Jew, was forced to herd pigs for a Gentile master. He was hungry and longed for the food the pigs were given. Eventually, he remembered his father's house and its well-laid tables. He decided to return and beg forgiveness. The father had all the while hoped for his son's return. When he saw the young man coming he ran to embrace him after calling out to the servants to fetch fresh clothes and to kill the fatted calf, for they would celebrate the return of his son. Later the elder son returned from working in the fields and, on hearing the cause for the music and rejoicing, he was filled with resentment. He entered the house where he accused his father of acting unjustly.

This is a Jewish parable invented and told by Jesus, a Jew. In this story the forgiving father represents God while the sons represent two aspects of sin. God is always waiting to forgive, but for the process to begin the sinner must first repent. Repentance is inseparable from forgiveness; without repentance there is no forgiveness. Yet from the Lucan tradition also come the words of Jesus on the cross: 'Father, forgive them, for they do not know what they are doing' (Lk. 23:34 NIV). These words keep ringing in the ears of Christians, who are likely to feel guilt if they fail to forgive another even when no repentance or desire for forgiveness is shown.

One night some years ago at the synagogue on Adelaide Road in Dublin, members of the Jewish-Christian Association discussed the question of forgiveness. It was a very relevant topic considering the situation in the north. The Jews present explained that for them John Paul II's forgiveness of his would-be assassin was meaningless, as was the late Gordon Wilson's forgiveness of the IRA members who had bombed his daughter Marie to death in Enniskillen. In neither case had repentance been shown or forgiveness sought. Forgiveness, they said, implies the restoration of right relationship, it could not be a one-sided affair. So what were the Christians about? During the discussion it was agreed that in many cases when a Christian forgave, the offender did not change. What happened was that the person who forgave was cleansed of resentment and of any desire for revenge, and was thus freed to move on from the situation and live life renewed.

In women's groups I have met people who reached a stage when they wished to be rid of guilt, blame or resentment in a particular relationship. In group prayer they would express their readiness to forgive but, not content with inner freedom, they would write, phone or visit the person who had offended them and so provoke further distressful reactions. There were also happier outcomes. However, in all cases when Christians are prepared to offer unsought forgiveness they need to act with tact and sensitivity. So where does this leave us in our approach to prayer? When sin is committed through offending another then repentance has to be expressed, not to God in a vacuum but through the one offended. If forgiveness is refused then the problem is no longer one's own. Likewise, if the offence has been committed against oneself and, desiring to be free of bitterness, one lets the other know of one's willingness to forgive, I believe the disposition essential for prayer is present. Reconciliation does not necessarily include a return to a close or working relationship, but rather a general sense of mutual goodwill towards each other.

The students of Cornelia Connelly College in the south-east of Nigeria took this Gospel teaching seriously. If two of them were 'keeping mute', that is refusing to speak to each other, they would not approach the altar for Holy Communion. Once, when a prefect reported such a situation, we sent for the two girls concerned. No, they were neither willing to repent nor to forgive. Were they prepared to pray for the grace to repent and forgive? No. Were they prepared to pray for the grace to desire the grace to repent and forgive? I have forgotten how many removes back we had to go! But finally, right relationships were restored. The point is, of course, that one's first approach to prayer may be to ask for the desire to desire to repent or to forgive.

According to Gospel teaching, prayer is concerned with developing attitudes of mind that transform our whole way of life. In his parable about two men at prayer in the Temple, Jesus described the teacher of religion listing his own virtues and thanking God for them. The tax-collector beat his breast in repentance and with few words expressed his vulnerability and dependence on God empowering him. Jesus commended this attitude while condemning the teacher's self-righteousness and implied judgment of others. Jesus made it clear both by teaching and example that private prayer entered into in trust and openness to the Spirit is essential for spiritual growth. It requires few words but a mind filled with goodwill towards others and a readiness to rid oneself of all hatred and resentment. In fact, Jesus went further and asked his disciples to wish well to their enemies and to pray for those who persecuted them. Finally, there was the occasion when Jesus arrived down from Mount Tabor and found the disciples trying in vain to heal an epileptic boy. When working in union with the faith of the boy's father Jesus healed the child, the disciples asked why they had not succeeded and Jesus told them prayer was needed. The teaching is clear: through our prayerful communion with God, others can be healed.

PRAYER IN THE SPIRIT
In the early church great emphasis was placed on praying with and through the Spirit. 'Pray in the Spirit at all times in every prayer and supplication' (Eph. 6:18 NRSV). 'Likewise the Spirit helps us in our weakness; for we do not know how to pray as we ought, but that very Spirit intercedes with sighs too deep for words' (Rom.

8:26 NRSV). 'Do not quench the Spirit. Do not despise the words of the prophets, but test everything; hold fast to what is good; abstain from every form of evil' (1 Thes. 5:19–22 NRSV). In his letter, James commends prayer on behalf of others saying, 'The prayer of a good person has a powerful effect' (James 5:16 GNB). He also recommends that we pray when in sorrow, but when happy to sing.

PAUSE FOR REFLECTION
The first part of this chapter was about listening; the second part was about prayer. In one sentence explain the connection between the two topics.

EXERCISE 1

How were your listening skills formed in your childhood home? (Were there constant arguments with everyone talking together or was it a matter of sulking silences? Did elders lecture and were children expected to keep quiet? Were meals spent watching TV or talking to each other, etc?)

What quality of listening goes on now in your adult home?

How were you made aware that you were not being listened to? (Did the person continue what she or he was doing? Did the person fail to make eye contact, start looking around, yawn, interrupt? Think of other signs you are aware of.)

When have you responded to another in the same way? (Was it when you did not like the person, did not agree with the mind-set, found the person dogmatic, were embarrassed by the topic, the person hogged the conversation and would not let others speak? Any other reasons?)

EXERCISE 2

How would developing the skill of listening attentively to others affect your prayer?

Prayer has been described as, 'Wasting time with God.' What are your thoughts on this approach to prayer?

EXERCISE 3

Complete the following sentences.

Prayer for me is . . .

I pray because . . .

I pray by . . .

When I pray I feel . . .

After prayer I . . .

AN EVENING REFLECTION

Of all the approaches to prayer, the one many people have found at first to be the most transformative is that of reflecting on the day's events and looking ahead to the morrow.

Sit comfortably and close your eyes.

Cast your mind back over the past twenty-four hours and watch yourself live through the day as though watching a film. Note where you met goodness in others today, and when you experienced goodness in yourself.

Check if you were aware of the Spirit's presence today. Did you at any point resist the Spirit's promptings?

Recall any thought or action you regret and express your sorrow. Note if there is someone to whom you wish to apologise or to act more positively towards.

Thank God for any event of the day for which you feel grateful. Again note if there is someone you wish to thank personally.

Now, let go of the day. Entrust it to the compassionate justice of God and be sure to retain no vestige of guilt or other negative feeling.

Still sitting comfortably, let your mind run ahead and see yourself living out the next day with its usual routine and anticipated events.

If there is something you fear or dislike about it see yourself live through it and ask the Spirit to empower you.

Recall each person you expect to meet tomorrow, family members, neighbours, colleagues, friends, etc. Ask to regard each one with the compassionate respect of Christ.

Then ask the Spirit to be with you in the unexpected whether it comes in the form of a joy or a sorrow.

Rest for a while and ask to be spiritually strengthened.

CLOSING THOUGHT

This evening recollection can take as little as seven minutes. In order to become whole, we need to use our human faculty of reflection and so become more responsible for our lives. Cornelia Connelly, the foundress of the Society of the Holy Child Jesus, when instructing our first sisters insisted:

'It is precisely because you are called to live busy lives, that you must lead a life of prayer.'[2]

11

RESURRECTION PEOPLE

OUR SPIRITUAL DIMENSION

In the opening pages of Chapter 1, mention was made of the women who accompanied Jesus during his public life. According to Luke some of these women had been healed by Jesus of various kinds of mental illness or diseases. Was the woman cured of her haemorrhage or the woman enabled to stand upright among them? It is recorded that after Jesus healed Peter's mother-in-law 'she began ministering to them' (Mk 1:31 Knox). By the time this Gospel was written, thirty or more years after the death of Jesus, this phrase apparently had acquired an ecclesial meaning, which suggests that Peter's mother-in-law became an active disciple. It would seem that these women had known suffering and some may even have been rejected by society. They could empathise with Jesus when in their presence he met with hostility, was called a drunkard and a glutton, and was accused of being mad or possessed.

These women for the most part, had grasped the fact that Jesus was challenging the authority structures developed among his people. In his community there were to be no status privileges, all were to strive in common to empower and serve each other. However, there was at least one woman who took longer than the others to understand this teaching. She is nameless, known only as the wife of Zebedee, or the mother of James and John. Hers is an interesting case. Was she a woman who lived through her sons? When James and John followed Jesus, leaving their father Zebedee to continue his fishing with hired men, she apparently went too. Then one day as Jesus and his disciples, women and men, were making their way to Jerusalem, she approached Jesus with her two sons, and asked him to promise that when he was made king he would give the two most senior posts to her boys!

Uncharacteristically, Jesus did not answer her directly but turned to the two young men and told them that they had failed to understand the suffering entailed in promoting God's reign. He made it clear that he had no privileges to bestow. The rest of the twelve were angry with the brothers; then Jesus once again explained that authority did not give one power over another but rather obliged one to serve for the good of others (see Mt. 20:20–28).

This time this unnamed disciple learned her lesson well and showed that she could face up to the suffering foretold, for later when her two sons fled she did not go with them but continued to follow Jesus all the way to Calvary. 'Many women were also there, looking on from a distance; they had followed Jesus from Galilee and had provided for him. Among them were Mary Magdalene, and Mary the mother of James and Joseph, and the mother of the sons of Zebedee' (Mt. 27:55–56 NRSV).

THE WOMEN WITNESSES

After the death of Jesus, Joseph, a member of the high priest's council who was a secret disciple of Jesus and who had not agreed with the decision to have him killed, risked going to Pilate and asking permission to take the body of Jesus down from the cross. Nicodemus, another councillor, went with him. They wrapped the body in linen and laid it in a rock tomb. The women disciples were there and saw where the body of Jesus was placed. It was Friday evening.

Throughout the Sabbath all remained quiet, except that the high priest and his council went to Pilate and asked to have the tomb guarded, for fear the disciples would take away the body of the Nazarene and then declare that he had risen. With Pilate's permission they sealed the tomb and set guards to watch. Unlike the disciples, they had remembered and had taken seriously Jesus' prophecy that he would rise on the third day.

At dawn on that first Easter morning, after the Sabbath had ended, the women disciples set out with jars of fragrant oils and spices in order to anoint the body of Jesus. On arriving they found the tomb open with the stone rolled back. All four Gospels record that the women were the first to discover the empty tomb. From this point on, the four accounts differ. Mark (the earliest of the four), says that on entering the tomb the women saw a young man who told them Jesus was risen and had left a message for the disciples to meet him in Galilee. The women ran from the tomb and told no one, because they were afraid. A later ending to Mark's account says that the women went to Peter and the other disciples and told of all they had seen and heard.

Luke records that two men appeared in dazzling clothes and the women bowed down before them in fear. The men asked,

> Why do you look for the living among the dead? He is not here; he has risen! Remember how he told you, while he was still with you in Galilee: 'The Son of Man must be delivered into the hands of sinful men, be crucified and on the third day be raised again.' Then they remembered his words. (Lk. 24:5–8 NIV)

They remembered for they had been among the intimates to whom Jesus had foretold his death and resurrection. The women returned to where the eleven and the rest of the disciples were gathered. They reported their findings and what the men had said to them. But the disciples regarded the women as foolish and did not believe them. Peter meanwhile ran to the tomb, saw that the body of Jesus had gone and returned filled with awe.

The Matthean account is similar, only this time it is an angel who tells the women that Jesus has risen. The women were hurrying from the tomb in fear and joy, when suddenly Jesus stood before them. Bowing down they clung to his feet. Then he told them to go and tell the disciples he would see them in Galilee. This is the first mention of the encounter between the risen Christ and the women.

It is hard to discover the exact relationship that existed between the men and women disciples. Jesus was constantly having to overcome the men's resistance as he endeavoured to communicate with women. First, it was the women with their children who were turned away until Jesus forbade it. Then it was the Canaanite woman as she called after him. His encounter with the Samaritan woman met with their disapproval, and Jesus had to speak up for the woman who anointed his feet. These women who were the trusted and loyal followers of Jesus met with rejection and scorn. Later the risen Christ rebuked the eleven: 'He scolded them, because they did not have faith and because they were too stubborn to believe those who had seen him alive' (Mk 16:14 GNB).

Neither Mark nor Luke record the encounter between the risen Christ and this group of women disciples, perhaps because in

Jewish law women had no legal status as witnesses. But the risen Christ had ignored this rule for, in his community, heralding a new way of relating, there were to be no such status differences.

MARY OF MAGDALA

The fourth Gospel was written around AD 100; that is, about seventy years after the death of Jesus. In AD 70, the Romans had destroyed the Temple, and the Jews, fearful for their own safety, banished the Jewish Christians from their synagogues. So for three decades the early church was on its own, suffering several persecutions, as it reflected on and developed its understanding of Jesus and the mission entrusted to its care.

The resurrection account as recorded by the Johannine community gives great prominence to the witness of Mary of Magdala. Magdala was a commercial town situated by the Sea of Galilee. When mentioning the women who stood by the cross, Matthew, Mark and John name Mary of Magdala but do not introduce her as they do the other women. Presumably, therefore, she was well known in church circles by the end of the century.

In this later account Mary Magdalene alone is mentioned as going to the tomb and discovering it empty, though when she reported the fact to Peter she used the term *we*. She then followed Peter and another disciple back to the tomb. On finding the body gone, the men returned to the other disciples while Mary remained by the tomb weeping. Suddenly a man standing beside her asked, 'Woman, why are you weeping? Whom are you looking for?' She thought it was the gardener until the man called her by name; then she recognised Jesus.

> Jesus said to her, 'Do not hold on to me, because I have not yet ascended to the Father. But go to my brothers and say to them, "I am ascending to my Father and your Father, to my God and your God."' Mary Magdalene went and announced to the disciples, 'I have seen the Lord'; and she told them that he had said these things to her. (Jn 20:15, 17–18 NRSV)

In a commentary on this incident, Teresa Okure complains that the significance of Mary's role is ignored while commentators focus on the words, 'Do not hold on to me.' These words are compared to the invitation given to Thomas to come and place his finger in the wounds inflicted on Jesus. The conclusion reached is that the risen Christ did not want to be defiled by the touch of a woman.[1]

Such an interpretation is not in keeping with the Jesus whom women have come to know in the Gospels.

Jesus did not tell Mary to proclaim that he was risen from the dead. That information was given by the angels. He commissioned her to repeat his message, 'I am ascending to my Father and your Father, to my God and your God.' This is the good news. We are the children of God, sisters and brothers of the risen Christ, and of each other. Paul grasped this fundamental truth and wrote: 'There is no longer Jew or Greek, there is no longer slave or free, there is no longer male or female; for you are one in Christ Jesus' (Gal. 3:28 NRSV).

Continuing her commentary, Teresa Okure writes:

> This is the primary and foundational Easter message. Mary is, therefore, not simply an apostle of apostles; she was commissioned by the risen Jesus himself to bear and proclaim the message of messages to the disciples. This message, which concerns the significance of Jesus' resurrection for believers, their common parenthood in and brotherhood/sisterhood in Christ, sums up the entire purpose of Jesus' mission and God's work of salvation. . . .
>
> . . . The NT evidence shows that the early Christians took this message seriously to heart and transformed it into a programme of action: they designated one another as brothers and sisters and forged a communitarian way of life to enable them to live out this new relationship. Thus they ensured that none of their brothers or sisters were ever in want (cf. Acts 2:43–46; 4:32–37). The Johannine community and Paul in particular emphasised the wonder of this new identity and urged their members to show that they are indeed children of God by loving one another as God loves them.[2]

Mary of Magdala was the first to experience the resurrection faith, that the risen Christ is present in the guise of others. Because the gardener called her by name, showed concern for her and treated her with respect, she was able to recognise the presence of Christ and say, 'I have seen the Lord.'

Mary of Magdala was held in high esteem by the early church. During the first three centuries Irenaeus, Origen and Chrysostom wrote of her as a disciple of Jesus and a prime witness to the resurrection. Contemporary Gnostic writings gave her a prominent role in the early Christian community. However, there is a marked difference between the Mary of Magdala as presented in the Gospels and the later Christian tradition that developed around the Magdalene.

It is believed that Augustine in the fifth century started the confusion between Mary of Magdala and the unknown prostitute who anointed the feet of Jesus. It is suggested that Augustine, repenting of his past sexual indulgence, found solace in the thought of the repentant prostitute becoming a loyal follower of Jesus and chosen witness of his resurrection. Others point out that the confusion was caused by the fact that Luke followed his account of the anointing by immediately introducing the group of women disciples led by Mary Magdalene, out of whom Jesus had cast seven demons. In the popular mind demons came to be associated with sexual immorality. Scripture scholars explain that prostitutes were referred to as sinners, while possession by demons referred to mental or physical disorders.

By AD 600, Gregory the Great was referring to Mary Magdalene as the 'repentant sinner'. During the following centuries artists delighted in portraying Mary of Magdala as a voluptuous young woman, swooning by the cross of Jesus. Such a portrayal is not Gospel. By the twelfth century Bernard of Clairvaux bestowed on her the title 'Apostle to the Apostles'. Yet artists continued to employ beautiful young models to represent a woman whose sufferings would have drained her of all such youthful beauty.

A third tradition developed in medieval France when Mary of Magdala was identified with Mary of Bethany, sister of Martha and Lazarus. The myth which prevailed was that Mary Magdalene, together with Martha and Lazarus, had to flee from Palestine and eventually arrived in the south of France where Lazarus was made bishop! A thirteenth-century window in the Cathedral of Auxerre depicts Mary Magdalene preaching.

When the risen Christ commissioned Mary of Magdala to proclaim the good news he told her to 'go to my brothers and tell them', etc. He used the term *adelphoi* which apparently is the plural for siblings of both sexes. Yet Mary interpreted Christ as meaning the community of disciples, not that of his family. To the Jew the word 'brethren' meant fellow-Jews, but as the significance of Christ's message became clear to these first Jewish Christians they were able to accept and break bread with their Gentile sisters and brothers.

Concluding her analysis of the good news entrusted to Mary of Magdala, Teresa Okure writes:

> Fidelity to our relationship to one another as brothers and sisters in Christ demands that we eschew all activities that smack of superiority and inferiority complexes. . . . In the socio-economic and political spheres, the challenge of Mary Magdalene's commission will move the so-called Christian countries of the west to care for their less fortunate sisters and brothers in the two-thirds world. . . . More especially, the recognition that we are all brothers and sisters in Christ will help towards according to women their rightful place in church and society. . . . In particular this will demand that the church listens to the witness of women to Christ today, that it takes seriously the commission that they alone can declare to be what they have received from Christ for the good of the community.[3]

In other words, those exercising authority in the church need to listen to women as they witness to their experience of Christ at work in their lives. The acceptance of the women's witness will benefit the whole community.

OUR SPIRITUAL DIMENSION

The resurrection reminds us of another aspect of our human existence. It is the spiritual dimension that leaves us with a restless yearning, a sense that there is yet more to discover as to what it means to be fully human and that death is but a part of the human span. Long before Jesus, Eastern cultures and faiths had directed their energies towards gaining this enlightenment.

Today physicists tell us that humankind, in keeping with evolutionary patterns, has now reached the required number of people on earth to provide the mass brain power needed for the next quantum leap. Not only is the brain power in place, but so also is the network of communication technology that can carry new ideas instantly around the globe. They predict that the next stage of human development will concentrate on our spiritual dimension and lead us further into the realm of the mystery we call God.[4]

The human spirit is that part of us which can transcend our bodily limitations through mind and will and finds fulfilment in divine empowerment. Over and over again people have tried to define their awareness of its reality, but finally it has to be recognised through our external behaviour. Each culture is leavened by its own spirituality, its own search for the source and meaning of life.

There are always temptations awaiting those who believe in the spiritual dimension. One temptation is to seek spiritual consolation and comfort rather than divine empowerment, to remain passive and interpret unjust situations as 'the will of God'. Another temptation is to allow one's life to become compartmentalised so that religious devotions have little influence on one's political, economic or social values.

For Jesus a true spirituality is integrated into the whole of life and its active presence can be recognised through a person's actions. Jesus lived a fully human life, sharing the limitations imposed upon us by gender, race, culture, health and time. He was a member of a family, and of a rural and religious community. He practised a trade, attended social gatherings, and sought solitude. He experienced family tension, relaxed with friends, and inspired great devotion from his followers. Throughout it all, his spirituality empowered and integrated the whole of his life on earth.

The development of our spiritual dimension demands first that we become more intensely aware of the fact that we are alive. The sinner has been likened to an arrow off course. To be given the gift of life, provided with a time span and yet not to have achieved the fullness of human life is seen by some as the greatest sin. The story is told of a Zen master who when asked what enlightenment had done for him said, 'When I hear, I hear; when I see, I see; when I taste, I taste; when I touch, I touch.' True spirituality enables us to understand the familiar in a new way. Explaining the Franciscan approach to spirituality Brother Ramon writes:

> By 'Franciscan spirituality' is meant a way of believing, of experiencing, of living and sharing in the wonder of creation and in the fullness of the gospel. It is a way in which the salt is present and active, giving a distinctive taste and sustaining power, and preserving life from insipidness and corruption.[5]

A LOVE FULL OF ACTION

The Incarnation was a missionary undertaking, a love full of action. In keeping with his mission Jesus concentrated on individuals challenging them to undergo an inner conversion. Frequently he sought out and associated with sinners, those who had gone off-course. He constantly reiterated the teaching conveyed in the words of the prophet Micah when he declared:

> this is what Yahweh asks of you:
> only this, to act justly,
> to love tenderly
> and to walk humbly with your God. (Mi. 6:8 JB)

Jesus described the divine welcome awaiting those who live out this teaching as follows: 'Come. . . . For I was hungry and you gave me food; I was thirsty and you gave me drink; I was a stranger and you made me welcome; naked and you clothed me, sick and you visited me, in prison and you came to see me' (Mt. 25:34–36 JB). And just as these people described by Jesus did not recognise the fact that in serving their neighbour they had entered the Christ dimension, so I have met 'born' Catholics who never associated their work among prisoners, their involvement in the women's movement, or their contributions at a shareholder's meeting as having anything to do with promoting God's reign of peace and justice on earth.

Promoting justice with compassion is the essential core of Christian discipleship. One Sunday afternoon in 1957 when travelling by car in eastern Nigeria the fuel in the tank ran low. The driver called in to the nearest mission station to collect a can of petrol. While waiting I sat with four university students, all men, who were holding a Bible session. They focused on the text: 'Very truly, I tell you, the one who believes in me will also do the works that I do and, in fact, will do greater works than these, because I am going to the Father' (Jn 14:12 NRSV). They had no problem in accepting the word of Jesus at face value, nor in committing themselves to continue his work of challenging, of peace-making and of bringing healing to others. It was then I realised that my faith practice was too devotionally based, too geared to the observance of religious regulations and to passing them on to others. Though of an age with these young men who were new to Christianity, I did not yet have their trust in the power of the Spirit at work in me.

Forty years later in 1997 I was with a group of twelve Catholics in Dublin. Some were Nigerian, some Irish and we ranged in age from twenty-six to sixty-six. We had met to explore together what it meant to be a disciple of Jesus today. After some sharing of ideas, each in turn expressed his or her understanding of Christian discipleship. It turned out that each of us held one or other of the two views that emerged. For some, being a Christian meant loving Jesus as a friend, frequently setting aside time for prayer, and for his sake being kind to others. The rest believed that Christian commitment called them to challenge injustices in church and society, and empowered by the Spirit to be prepared to take risks to promote God's reign of peace on earth.

Sitting in with us was a young Moslem recently arrived from the Middle East. He had known Jesus only through the *Koran,* but the week before our meeting he had read the Gospel according to Matthew. While the various views were being written up on a flip-chart he offered his. This is what he said: 'To be a follower of Jesus, you would have to be very kind and very honest.' Coming fresh to the Gospel he had seen clearly the approach of Jesus, justice with compassion, and in one short sentence summed up the two approaches taken by the others present. Immediately my mind went back to those young men on a Nigerian verandah and I prayed silently that we might always approach the Gospels with fresh eyes and a clear mind.

The work of today's missionaries, as they cross cultures and religions, accompanying and being accompanied by those they meet, is likened to beggars sharing with each other where to find bread. Asian women say that following Jesus is not a lonely path but a collective enterprise. They realise that the Western missionaries' interpretation of the Gospel cannot be the yardstick by which they measure the truth of their own people's spiritual experience. In theology today they say, 'We are the text.'[6] This is true for most women, many of whom have yet to identify the Spirit active in their own experiences.

Rosemary Edet writes:

> Contemporary church women, taking a clue from their forebears in the Gospels, have felt impelled by the Spirit to respond to human needs, not only in the personal expression of prayer or in interpersonal spheres of immediate care and concern, but in the public domain. . . . They undertake advocacy roles for the poor, the prisoners, for the dependent and helpless battered women and men. Whether through Catholic organizations or in a federal or state office or staff position or in a public interest capacity, women undertake to put into practice the goal of Christian action. . . .

Furthermore, women in our churches are disaffected because these churches represent power relationships and because this power is often insensitively administered. Many women have discovered talents in themselves for building the Christian community but they cannot use these because they are women. . . . The ministry of justice involves them in confrontation with the powers of the church and state and business establishments.[7]

Just as Mary Magdalene and her companions were called foolish and not believed, so today the risen Christ continues to work through unlikely people. It requires the gift of faith to recognise his presence. Each day broken and damaged people prove to be a source of grace and healing for others. Many of us will be able to recall gaining new insights and renewed hope from the most unexpected quarters, and even more surprisingly will have discovered that when we were at our lowest, darkest moments the Christ Spirit touched others through us. So with confidence we can pray the great prayer of Saint Francis:

Lord, make me an instrument of your peace;
where there is hatred let me sow love.
Where there is injury, pardon; where there is doubt, faith,
and where there is despair, hope.

PAUSE FOR REFLECTION
Recall a time, perhaps as a child, when you were disbelieved, considered foolish, felt rejected. Allow the feelings you felt then arise in you again.

Recall a time when you disbelieved or scorned another, even someone speaking on TV. What factual evidence had you to justify your attitude?

How would you like to be treated when you make a statement?

How would you like to react to others when they make a statement?

Is your practice of the faith a response to the Gospel call, or to a personal need for devotional comfort?

What do you consider to be the strengths and weaknesses of your Christian community? How do you contribute to either?

EXERCISE 1

List aspects of the Christian churches today that you think Jesus would recognise as the continuance of his reform movement.

List any aspect that you believe he would challenge.

EXERCISE 2

Recall the past twenty-four hours.

Identify moments when you became aware of the spiritual 'you'.

Plan how best you can intensify this awareness.

Draw a symbol to represent your spiritual dimension.

Fix it to your mirror.

GOSPEL REFLECTION

Sit back and, whether you are a man or a woman, imagine yourself as one of the group of Galilean women who followed Jesus. Choose a particular occasion during your time with Jesus, e.g. when you first heard him preach, on the journey to Jerusalem, at the paschal supper, by the cross, or the encounter by the tomb. Stay with that incident for a while.

What difference did Jesus bring to your life as you journeyed with him?

Come into the present and place yourself in the presence of the risen Christ.

Explain how you interpret his Good News. Remain in silence.

Mention the prejudices and fears from which you feel the need to be freed.

Offer yourself as an instrument of the divine Spirit.

Specify a situation in which you are willing to strive to make the Good News a reality.

CLOSING THOUGHT

'We are our selves the only obstacle to the overflowing of Divine Love.' (Cornelia Connelly, Foundress of the Society of the Holy Child Jesus.)

12

Various approaches to prayer

And additional personal development exercises

In his letter to the Romans, Paul said that we do not know how to pray; therefore, the Spirit prays for and with us. However, there are several steps we can take in order to prepare for prayer. The first is to set aside a regular time for private recollection.

Meditation and contemplation

In the Western tradition, meditation means to exercise the mind. One reads a passage from Scripture, or a poem, or recalls the day's events and allows the mind to explore the implications for one's own life. From this process prayer may arise. The meditation itself is not regarded as prayer but as preparation for prayer, and can lead into contemplation when the mind no longer considers point after point but focuses on a single thought until one becomes aware of being in the divine presence and enters into silent communion through the Spirit. Confusion can be caused when discussing prayer with those from the Eastern tradition, for they sometimes refer to the mental exercise as contemplation and the silent communion as meditation.

Many people are not aware of their deep spiritual potential. The more we become aware of the inner transforming power of the spiritual through faith, hope and love, the more natural and human it becomes for us to enter into the mind of Christ and live lives of prayer acting in accordance with the known will of our Creator and Redeemer. Of course, there is ample scope here for self-deception. An old Irish custom called Ainm Cara (soul friend) dates back to the Celtic monks and is a great safeguard against any delusions. Two or more people gather together regularly and share their experience of prayer and its effect on their lives. None assumes the role of guru or spiritual director but all share in common. There are variations on this practice, with one person taking the role of listener and questioner but not sharing in return. The soul friend concept is one worth pursuing as we all need faith support during our time on earth.

While we can provide time for recollection, according to a 1995 *Encyclopedia of Catholicism*, the entrance into prayer itself depends on God's initiative. The word 'prayer' has the root meaning of petitioning. Being aware of our own needs and those of others is a good way to enter into the process. But prayer is not a process by which we try to manipulate God's will, rather it is we who are changed, and by developing our spiritual dimension we gain the insight and strength to understand and co-operate with God's will for us.[1]

ORAL PRAYER

In childhood many of us memorised a number of prayer formulas. These are always a great standby and source of comfort, especially when in sickness or old age we are unable to focus our thoughts. In my youth I learned what were called 'aspirations' and I still find myself using them. My favourite ones come from Scripture, but from which translation I do not know.

'Lord, that I may see' (Mk 10:51). 'Lord, he (she) whom thou lovest is sick' (Jn 11:3). 'Lord, if thou willest thou canst make me whole.' And the answer, 'I do will it, be thou made whole' (Mk 1:40–41).

INTERCESSORY PRAYER

Through our intercessions we express our dependence on the divine source of our being. Remember Jesus' instruction to use few words, for our real needs are already known. Simply recall the need and place it in silence before our all-empowering God. If you are praying for others, bring them to mind and place them in God's presence. Remain in silent company with the Godhead, that is, with the source of all being, who shares divinity with us; the eternal Word and redeeming Love who shared our humanity; and the Spirit who inspires and sustains us.

PRAYER THROUGH THE BODY AND ITS SENSES

All cultures and religions use special body postures when entering into prayer. The idea is to arrange the body structure in such a way as to afford the maximum comfort and so prevent the body from becoming a source of distraction. Some kneel upright, the back and head comfortably aligned. Others use the lotus position in which the upper body is comfortably supported by a solid base provided by the careful folding of the lower limbs. Today, many people prefer to sit and relax each muscle in turn, beginning with the scalp and going right down to the toes, then remaining for a while aware of their breathing rhythm until all mental preoccupations have ceased and they are ready to enter into prayer.

Movement is sometimes used while at prayer, by means of frequent bowing, or by alternating kneeling with prostration. Movement can express special acts of worship, such as kneeling with the head bowed in adoration, or standing with the arms raised in praise or supplication. These movements can be developed into dance. In each case the body posture becomes the silent means through which we enter into spiritual communion with the divine. In desolation and distress it is sometimes helpful to return to the foetal position. Kneel down and sit back between the feet, then bend forward and leave the head resting between the knees with the brow touching the floor. The arms are left relaxed along the sides of the body. Younger, more flexible bodies can hold this position for quite a while. Older, stiffer bodies need to modify the position. Through assuming the foetal position one is expressing total dependence and vulnerability before God.

Another popular preparation for prayer is to bring the mind totally into the present. Walk or sit and become aware of one's own breathing, of the light or darkness. Flex the muscles, hear the sounds of the wind, the rain, the birds, the traffic, the human footsteps and voices. Feel the clothes touching your skin, the ground under your feet, the heat of the sun or the cold in a breeze. Smell the flowers, the pollution, the animals. See the room, the buildings, the vehicles, the people and become aware of the divine presence. Speak to God as the heart dictates, then listen and let the thoughts and insights come.

In Bray, a seaside town south of Dublin, there lived an old man. Some friends of mine, a young couple who were members of the St Vincent de Paul Society, called early one summer evening to bring him supplies for the weekend. They knocked and knocked until finally the old man appeared in his pyjamas and wanted to know why they were getting him up in the middle of the night. Surprised, they pointed to the sun. Then he brought them through to the back of his house which faced east. He pointed to a beautiful copper beech. 'I have to be up by 4 am' he explained, 'to watch the sun rise up behind that tree as it sets it aglow with golden light. To miss that sight would be an insult to God.'

BIBLE REFLECTION
The Bible is an endless source for reflection.

Recollect your thoughts.

When ready read slowly through your chosen text.

Go back over words or phrases that resonated with you by repeating them, each in turn.

Then once again read through the text.

Remain in silence allowing the Word to speak to you.

Ask: 'All-empowering Spirit, what do you want of me?'

Remain in silence.

Thank the Spirit for any insights received.

End by resolving to live a Gospel value relevant to the text.

BIBLE FANTASY
Those with active imaginations find it a help to enter into a Bible fantasy. Again, sit comfortably and relax for a few moments; then as before read slowly through the chosen scene.

Read the passage a second time.

Closing your eyes enter into the scene, identifying with one of the characters. It may be Jesus himself, a disciple, a Pharisee, a member of the crowd, or you may decide to remain as yourself and become a silent observer.

When ready (five, fifteen or thirty minutes later), return to the present.

Stay in silence savouring the experience.

Speak to God.

Give thanks for any insights received.

Decide if there is any action you should take in response to the experience.

THE ROSARY

Another form of Bible reflection practised by Roman Catholics is called the Rosary. Tradition tells us that it was given in the thirteenth century by St Dominic to illiterate Christians in order to help them keep in mind the main events in the life of Christ. It remains a popular preparation for prayer today, though many devotees no longer use it as a Bible reflection; some are not even aware that there are a set number of Gospel events to recall. These events are divided into three sets of five. The five joyful mysteries are recalled on Mondays and Thursdays and remind us that God became incarnate. The five sorrowful mysteries are meditated on Tuesdays and Fridays and recall the suffering and death of Jesus. The five glorious mysteries remind us that Christ is risen and are recalled on Wednesdays, Saturdays and Sundays. Of course, one can choose other events to remember. Rosary beads are available to aid in timing the meditations. The usual pattern for these is a circlet of fifty beads separated into five sets of ten. Each set is called a decade and between each decade is a single larger bead. Usually a small crucifix is suspended from the circlet. It is possible to get a one decade rosary bracelet, and also a rosary ring surrounded with ten small knobs. On each bead of the decade a 'Hail Mary' is recited slowly, thus marking the length of time allowed for recalling each Gospel event. The slow recitation of the 'Hail Mary' over and over has been compared to the musical accompaniment to a song, which in this case is the mystery meditated, each event providing, as it were, a new verse. At the close of each meditation when the single large bead is reached the 'Our Father' is recited. When undertaken by a praying group, the Rosary can become quite a ceremony. The Gospel events can be read aloud, each followed by a short reflection also made aloud, with perhaps a special petition assigned to each decade.

THE PRAYER OF SILENCE

When the prophet Elijah fled from his enemies he arrived at Mount Horeb and there waited for God to speak to him. The Bible tells us that Elijah did not hear God in the storm that split the rocks, nor in the earthquake, nor in the fire that followed, but in the sound of sheer silence (see 1 Kgs 19:11–12). Later the psalmist would convey the same truth in the line, 'Be still, and know that I am God' (Ps. 46:10 NRSV). Various approaches have been devised in order to achieve the inner silence in which one may become aware of the promptings of the Spirit. Some gaze on an Icon or picture. Others use a mantra, that is, a word or phrase repeated slowly until the mind is brought to quiet rest and is able to focus on the reality of being in the divine presence. The Jesus Prayer is an ancient form of the prayer of silence much practised by Eastern Christians. The mantra they use is, 'Jesus Christ, Son of the living God, have mercy on me, a sinner.' The whole supplication is repeated several times. Then gradually some words are dropped beginning with the end phrase 'a sinner', until finally only the name 'Jesus' remains. When at last the holy name ceases to be repeated the person remains in silence for the rest of the period, focusing only on the fact that one is present to the Godhead.

PAUSE FOR REFLECTION
In Chapter 2 we met a man part paralysed and a woman bowed down who, on being touched by Jesus, became physically whole and faced a new, changed way of life. So too when empowered by the Christ Spirit inner change becomes part of our lives. There are certain givens that cannot be changed such as our inherited genes, race, cultural and religious upbringing, family, schooling, illnesses, accidents and so on. What we can change is our response to past influences and present situations.

Aware of this reality, a mystic of old prayed, 'Lord, give me the grace to change what can be changed; the serenity to accept that which cannot be changed; and the wisdom to know the difference.'

EXERCISE 1

1. Specify and list the givens in your life.

   Underline those which could benefit from a change of attitude.

2. List people who keep you passive or negative towards yourself.

   Decide whether it is wiser to avoid them for the present, or to take a new approach towards them.

3. List situations that make you feel negative.

   Judge whether you can avoid them, or need to approach them more confidently.

4. Recall the past twenty-four hours.

   Did you blame, fault-find or put-down yourself or another unnecessarily?

If so, resolve to be more positive towards yourself and others tomorrow.

EXERCISE 2

1. On separate slips of paper write down a prejudice, grudge, false expectation or low opinion of self that keeps you from living fully.

2. Then take up each slip one at a time, read what you have written and smile at yourself.

3. Now tear the papers in half and dispose of them.

GOSPEL REFLECTION

One day when Jesus was beside the Sea of Galilee teaching, Jairus, the leader of the local synagogue, came to him. Throwing himself at the feet of Jesus he begged him to come and heal his daughter who was at the point of death. Immediately, Jesus rose and went with Jairus. The people followed. Before they reached the house, messengers came saying it was too late as the girl was already dead. Jesus encouraged Jairus to believe. Then with Peter, James and John he entered the house. There he found the family and friends distressed and weeping, but when he said the child was not dead but only sleeping they laughed at him. The parents led Jesus to where the girl lay, and taking her by the hand he said, 'Talitha, cumi', which means, 'Maiden, I say to thee, rise up' (Mk 5:42 Knox). Immediately the girl stood up and began to walk about. Jesus told the parents to give her some food. For Jesus food signified new life. The girl was twelve years of age and about to enter into womanhood (Mk 5:21–24, 35–43).

As Jesus continued on his way he saw me sitting listlessly. He stopped and gazed into my eyes, taking me by the hand he called me by name ' . . . . ' Then he said, 'Arise, you are not dead but sleeping.' I stood upright. Jesus said, 'Fear not. Only believe, and all will be well.' He invited me to join his company and his companions immediately shared their bread with me.

Later, alone with Jesus I said, ' Jesus, I . . . .
. . . .
. . . .
. . . . ,
. . . . '
(continue in quiet conversation and silence).

FINAL EXERCISE:
As a result of reading this book, list:

1. Anything new you learned about Jesus.

2. Anything new you learned about yourself.

3. Any ideas you disagree with.

4. Any facts or ideas you found empowering.

5. Any ideas that left you feeling uncertain.

6. Any ideas you would like to explore further.

7. Any changes you would like to make in your present lifestyle.

FURTHER GOSPEL REFLECTIONS
Throughout the Gospels Jesus is constantly recorded as asking questions. Take the following questions one at a time and answer Jesus in your own words.

1. Will you also leave me? (Jn 6:67)

2. Woman, why are you weeping? (Jn 20:15)

3. Why are you frightened? Where is your faith? (Mk 4:40)

4. Do you want to be made whole? (Jn 5:6)

5. Why do you notice the speck in another's eye and ignore the log in your own? (Lk. 6:41)

6. Whom do you say that I am? (Lk. 9:20)

7. Who are my brothers? (Mk 3:33)

8. Do you love me? (Jn 21:17)

9. Give me to drink? (Jn 4:7)

10. How much bread have you got? (Mk 8:5)

FINAL THOUGHT
'Let that mind be in you which was in Christ Jesus' (Phil. 2:5).

NOTES

CHAPTER 1

1. Okure, Teresa SHCJ (1989), *A Theological View of Women's Role in Promoting Culture/Human Development*, AFER 31, No. 6. MECEA, Pastoral Inst. Eldoret, p. 366.
2. *Ibid.*, p. 367.
3. Edet, Rosemary HHCJ (1992), 'Women and Evangelisation', *Evangelization in Africa in the Third Millennium*, Nigeria, Port Harcourt: CIWA Press, p. 129.
4. Oduyoye, Mercy (1994), 'Violence Against Women', *Journal of Inculturation Theology*, Vol. 1, No. 1, Port Harcourt, Nigeria: CIWA Press, p. 43.
5. Vatican Council II (Flannery ed.) (1996), *Pastoral Constitution of the Church in the Modern World*, a.7, Dublin: Dominican Publications, 1996.
6. Dreyer, Elizabeth (1995), 'Christian Spirituality', *Encyclopedia of Catholicism*, London: HarperCollins, p. 1219.
7. *Ibid.*, p. 1220.

CHAPTER 2

1. Nolan, Albert OP (1987), *Jesus Before Christianity*, London: Darton Longman and Todd, p. 117.

CHAPTER 3

1. Connelly, Cornelia, Foundress of the Society of the Holy Child Jesus, 1809–79.
2. Leonard, Richard SJ (1995), *Beloved Daughters*, Ottawa: Novalis, St Paul's University, p. 89.
3. Okure, Teresa SHCJ, (1993), *The Challenge of the Anointing of Jesus in Bethany for the Contemporary Church*, Nairobi: Kathohsche Jungscha, Oesteneichs et BICAM, p. 143.
4. *Ibid.*, p. 142.
5. *Ibid.*, p. 145.
6. Maher, Betty (1993), *Just a Thought*, RTE, 29 April.

7. Psalter of a Cistercian Convent in Basel, 1260, Municipal Library, Besancon.
8. Nolan, Christopher (1987), *Under the Eye of the Clock,* London: Weidenfeld and Nicolson, p. 38.

CHAPTER 4

1. Okure, Teresa SHCJ, at a Christology Workshop given to the Holy Child Sisters, in Mayfield, Sussex, July 1996.
2. *Ibid.*
3. Okure, Teresa SHCJ (1992), 'The Will to Arise', *Women, Tradition and the Church in Africa,* M. A. Oduyoye and M. R. A. Kanyoro, eds, p. 230.
4. Hyun Kyung, Chung (1991), *Struggle to be Sun Again,* London: SCM Press, p. 51.
5. Finnerty, Adam Daniel (1979), *No More Plastic Jesus,* New York, Maryknoll: Orbis Books, pp. 2–3.
6. de Mello, Anthony SJ (1996), *The Song of the Bird,* Anand, India: Gujarat Sahitya Prakash, pp. 150–51.
7. See Ira Progoff (1975) 'Dialogue with the Body', *At a Journal Workshop,* New York: Dialogue House Library, pp. 194–210.

CHAPTER 5

1. Okure, Teresa SHCJ, at a Christology Workshop given to the Holy Child Sisters, in Mayfield, Sussex, July 1996.
2. Edet, Rosemary HHCJ (1990) 'Women in Evangelisation', *Evangelisation in Africa in the Third Millennium,* Port Harcourt, Nigeria: CIWA Press, p. 129.
3. Oduyoye, Mercy (1994) 'Violence Against Women', *Journal of Inculturation Theology,* No. 1, Port Harcourt, Nigeria: CIWA Press, p. 47.
4. Okure, Teresa SHCJ, see Chapter 5, Note 1.

CHAPTER 6

1. ISPCC, Russel Court Hotel, Dublin, 8 May 1997.

CHAPTER 8

1. *Encyclopedia of Catholicism,* (1995), London: HarperCollins, p. 1193.
2. *The Church in the Modern World,* a.16.
3. Pope John Paul II, *Mullieris Dignitatem,* n.14, 1988.
4. Hyun Kyung, Chung (1990), *Struggle to be Sun Again,* SCM Press, p. 44.

CHAPTER 9

1. Pope John XXIII (1963), *Pacem in Terris,* a.41 and a.44, CTS.
2. *Modern Catholic Encyclopedia,* (1994), Glazier and Hellwig (eds), Dublin: Gill and Macmillan, p. 688.
3. *The Koran,* sura XXVII, Vs, 23, 33 and 34, (1974), translated by J. M. Rodwell, London: Everyman's Library, Dent.

4. *The New Jerome Biblical Commentary* (1995), London: Geoffrey Chapman, p. 374.

CHAPTER 10
1. *Constitutions of the Society of the Holy Child Jesus.* No. 24.
2. Connelly, Cornelia SHCJ (1959), *God Alone*, Burns and Oates, p. 45.

CHAPTER 11
1. Okure, Teresa SHCJ (1992), 'The significance of Jesus' Commission to Mary Magdalene', *The International Review of Mission* LXXXI/3, p. 177.
2. *Ibid.*, pp. 184–85.
3. *Ibid.*, pp. 187–88.
4. Peter Russel, from video entitled *The Global Brain*, and based on his book *The Awakening Earth* (1991), Penguin.
5. Brother Ramon (1994), *Franciscan Spirituality*, London: SPCK, p. 1.
6. See Chung Hyun Kyung (1991), *Struggle to be Sun Again*, SCM Press, pp. 97, 111.
7. Edet, Rosemary HHCJ (1990), 'Women and Evangelization', from *Evangelization in Africa in the Third Millennium*, Port Harcourt, Nigeria: CIWA Press, p. 132.

CHAPTER 12
1. *Encyclopedia of Catholicism* (1995), London: HarperCollins, pp. 1037–38.